M000300372

BANSHEES, BUGLES AND BELLES
TRUE GHOST STORIES
OF GEORGIA

Barbara Duffey

Rockbridge Publishing
an imprint of
HOWELL PRESS, INC.
Charlottesville, Virginia

Published by

Rockbridge Publishing
an imprint of
HOWELL PRESS, INC.
1713-2D Allied Lane
Charlottesville, VA 22903
(804) 977-4006
http://www.howellpress.com

A *Katherine Tennery Book*

Copyright 1995 by Barbara Duffey

All rights reserved. No part of this book may be reproduced in
any way or by any means without permission in writing from
Howell Press, Inc., with the exception of short passages for
review purposes.

Photographs copyright 1995 by the author with the exception of photos
on pages 3, 40, 43, and 47, which are used by permission of Louis Andrews.

Library of Congress Cataloging-in-Publication Data

Duffey, Barbara, 1943—
        Banshees, bugles and belles : true ghost stories of Georgia /
Barbara Duffey.
            p.   cm.
        Includes bibliographical references and index.
        ISBN 1-883522-08-0 (pbk.)
        1. Ghosts—Georgia.   2. Ghost stories, American—Georgia.
3. Haunted houses—Georgia.   I. Title.
GR110.G4D83   1995
398.2'09758'05—dc20   95-36423
                                                      CIP

08 07 06 05 04 03 02 01 00 99
10 9 8 7 6 5 4 3 2

TABLE OF CONTENTS

Acknowledgments v
Prologue vii

MILLEDGEVILLE

The Governor's Mansion 1
The Homestead 6
The Tate House 12
Maj. Edward White House 17
The Old State Capitol 20
Spirit of the Burial Mounds 23
Memory Hill Cemetery 24
Georgia College 29
The Ann Simpson Smith House 32
The House on Wilkinson Street 34
The Old State Prison 36
Culver Kidd's Drugstore 39
The Ghost of Marion Stembridge 42

MACON

The Hay House 51
The Beall House 61
St. James Church 68
The Woodruff House 72
Willingham Chapel 77
The Victorian House 80

PIEDMONT AND TIDEWATER

Ghosts at Tift College (Forsyth) 85
Panola Hall (Eatonton) 91
Ebenezer Swamp (Effingham County) 102
Col. George Fish House (Oglethorpe and Americus) 105
The Old Farm (Baxley) 109
Fort McAllister (Savannah) 111
Fort Pulaski (Savannah) 115

Bibliography 119
Interviews 123
Index 124

ACKNOWLEDGMENTS

Special thanks to Mauriel Joslyn for her support and guidance in the bibliographical research, to Linda Stewart, who edited the original draft, and to Erica Stewart, its first reader.

Many of the Milledgeville stories were contributed by family members, residents and visitors. I appreciate the support I received from the staff of the Governor's Mansion, especially Sandra Mason, Judson Barns and Alma Smith; A. Alling Jones and Linda Moore of the Georgia Military College; Binky Strickland, Greg Jarvie and Dr. Thomas Wilson of Georgia College. Randy Cannon, Mary Barbara Tate, Louis Andrews, Paul Campbell, Lorene Flanders, Ray Olivier and Sibley Jennings all contributed significantly. Elizabeth Kelly and the staff of the Mary Vincent Library were extremely helpful and cooperative. Special thanks to Charlie Edmonds of Central State Hospital.

In Macon my appreciation goes to the staff of the Washington Library; the family of Fran LaFarge, Kevin Cheek, Father and Mrs. Robert Gibson, the staff of the Mercer University Library Special Collections and Greg Mead. Norma Perkins and Thulia Bromlet were invaluable for their research on Leonidas Jordan. My appreciation goes out to the Confederate reenactors who helped with research.

My special thanks and appreciation to my family, who supported me in many ways while I worked on this book.

PROLOGUE

I never believed in ghosts until I moved into a lovely brick cape cod house in Baltimore, Maryland, with my seven-year-old son. The day we moved was hectic, but friends made the experience more tolerable.

I'll never forget the first night in the house. As soon as the sun went down, the house began to creak and moan, like thunder rolling across the living room ceiling, or kids running back and forth on the second floor—only there weren't any children up there. I kept asking my friends, "Doesn't it seem noisy in here to you?"

"It's a little noisy, but the house is settling," they assured me. I wasn't convinced, but I didn't know what else to think.

The noise eventually faded away that night, but it returned on and off for the next three days. Several times I heard the sound of footsteps on the stairs and coming into the kitchen. Not knowing what they were, I tried to ignore the unusual noises.

I was a little apprehensive, but for three months I managed to convince myself that it was nothing more than old house noises—until Halloween. At that time I didn't really understand the legend of All Hallow's Eve. On Halloween all of the spirits in the world, both good and evil, supposedly come out and walk around until midnight. At the stroke of twelve, the spirits return to their resting place until the next year.

That Halloween my son and I went trick-or-treating, but we were both safely in bed by ten o'clock. At 11:45 I was jarred awake by the horrendous sound of what seemed to be several bowling balls being rolled across the floor of the room above. I sat bolt upright and was startled by my black cat, who was sitting in front of the door and purring very loudly with his huge yellow eyes aglow. I was nearly frightened out of my wits, but forced myself to run downstairs to see if the noise was down there, too. I found the noise in the kitchen to be even more deafening—the pipes were clanking along with the rolling noises.

I called my best friend to see if she could hear the noises, and her reaction was powerful. "Get out of the house—NOW," she ordered. "It sounds like a volcano ready to blow up." I begged her to stay on the phone while I ran upstairs, my heart in my throat, to awaken my son. I practically dragged him down to the kitchen.

We stood outside on the back porch, as far away from the house as the phone cord would reach, listening to the horrible noises coming from inside. "Sell that house as soon as you can," my friend counseled. "Go tomorrow. Come over here to sleep tonight." I was so rattled that all I could think was how could I sell the house? I'd just moved in!

Then, just as suddenly as the noise began, it stopped. That horrific noise just stopped—as if nothing had happened. I looked at my watch, and it was exactly midnight.

My friend was still on the phone yelling, "You're crazy to stay there. Grab some things, and come over here. You've got to get away from there."

It was cold outside, and our feet were freezing. The kitchen looked all right to me. There was no green goo coming from the walls or anything like that. The cat strolled into the kitchen and meowed for food. I told my friend that it appeared the noise was gone. "I'll call you tomorrow."

"You'll be sorry," she said. "Get out of there."

I hung up, her warning ringing in my ear, but I was too tired to think about it any more. We walked around the house, but things seemed just fine. Nothing was out of place. It really did look as if nothing had ever happened, so we went to bed.

Nothing else happened that night. And except for a few footsteps now and then, nothing unusual happened. After a while, the noise on that Halloween night seemed like just a bad dream.

I almost forgot about the noises until nearly two years later, when the man I'd been dating asked me to marry him. I wondered how he'd react to the news that the house was haunted, and was relieved that he didn't make a big deal of it when I finally told him the story.

But after we were married and living in the house together, the noises began again. It seemed as if every time we had a disagreement, something in the house reacted. The heat vents resounded as if someone were banging on them.

At that point I researched the deed and discovered that the house had had seven owners. Each time the house was sold, the name on the deed was that of the wife, as the husband had either died or the couple had divorced. The only exception was the family who sold it to me, who had never hinted at any weirdness. Perhaps the spirit of one or more of the men who lived there sympathized with my husband.

We eventually sold the house and moved to a lovely, one-hundred-thirty-year-old, Shaker style farmhouse with acreage. After we'd been there for several days, we all remarked on how quiet the house was. There was never a sound—not a clanking pipe, nor throbbing heat vent, nor footsteps, nor thumps on the floor. There was never any unusual noise to make us suspicious of a spirit. Our old house was very noisy by comparison.

From that experience we learned two things: there are houses that are haunted, and there are houses that are not haunted. And so began my interest in ghosts.

The idea of spirits existing in a realm that we can't see has fascinated people from the beginning of time. The Bible has many verses attesting to eternal life, John 3:16 for example:

> For God so loved the world that he gave his only begotten
> son that whosoever believeth in him should not perish but
> have everlasting life.

But the Bible doesn't describe the life. What is it all about? When I think that some ghosts have haunted the same location for centuries, it makes me wonder. Jesus appeared many times after his death to his disciples. Maybe one of the reasons ghosts appear to us is to remind us of the existence of an afterlife.

I've heard that when a terrible tragedy occurs, the energy or magnetic field in that spot is disrupted, and the tragedy continues to play out for all eternity, like battlefields, or the site of a plane crash.

Whatever the reason for the spirits to manifest themselves, the Bible recognizes that there are both good and evil entities, as in I John 4:1-3:

> Dear friends, do not believe every spirit, but test the spirits to see whether they are from God, because many false prophets have gone out into the world. This is how you can recognize the spririt of God: Every spirit that acknowledges that Jesus Christ has come in the flesh is from God, but every spirit that does not acknowledge Jesus is not from God.

In searching for the answers to these questions, I've collected some very interesting stories, and I've tried very hard to document their truth. In most instances I've sought out more than one witness to tell you their stories. I hope you enjoy them. But if you are ever afraid, just pray:

> In the name of the Father, the Son Jesus, and the Holy Spirit, I ask for protection from any evil spirits.

I've been told that it will protect you from every kind of spirit.

MILLEDGEVILLE

THE GOVERNOR'S MANSION

The soft pink stucco mansion in the Greek Revival style at the corner of Clark and Hancock streets in Milledgeville was home to the governors of Georgia from 1838 until 1868. In 1864, during his infamous march to the sea, Union general William T. Sherman commandeered the mansion for his headquarters. Local legend says that displaced occupants knew the North had a great need of brass to make armaments, so all of the brass fixtures in the house—from the hinges to the window sash locks—were supposedly painted black to disguise their value and prevent pilferage.

The capital of Georgia was moved to Atlanta during Reconstruction, and the mansion was used as a boardinghouse until 1879, when it was pressed into use as dormitories for the Georgia Military and Agricultural College. From 1890 it served as the home of the presidents of Georgia College. Now that the mansion is open to the public for tours six days a week, intriguing hints of bygone days sometimes captivate visitors and museum personnel.

SOMETHING'S COOKING

On some cold mornings the welcoming odor of blueberry muffins cooking in the red-brick, walk-in fireplace in the kitchen tantalizes the visitor's sense of smell, but investigation finds the fireplace and stoves both empty and cold. At other times the smell of woodsmoke seems to permeate the lower level of the house, but no fire has burned there for years. Some say it must be Molly, a cook who worked all her life in the governor's mansion, still at work.

Some people claim that they can set their watch by the smells that emanate from the kitchen—Molly, who cooked for the agricultural college and the first Georgia College presidents, seems to serve dinner at precisely twelve noon and have supper ready at five in the evening. Some say they smell pork and black-eyed peas cooking every day of the year, yet others deny having ever smelled anything.

The smell of cigar and pipe smoke is often noted in the library, where the men were known to retire after dinner for their tobacco and brandy, yet no one has smoked there in recent times.

THE UNTIDY GHOST

Once, when guests stayed at the mansion, a servant went upstairs as usual to change the linen and make up the bed, after which he returned to the kitchen. Sometime later one of the residents discovered the bed unmade and the linen draped all over the floor. The puzzled servant returned to the room and made up the bed for the second time. To his great surprise, it was later discovered that the bedclothes were again disturbed, as if by a restless spirit. The servant made up the bed for a third time, swearing that he had completed his task in each instance. He was so frightened by this experience that he was reluctant to enter that bedroom ever again.

LIGHTS OUT!

In 1992, during one of the many tours that are conducted through the mansion, all the lights in the library flickered on and off, in some kind of mysterious cadence. The rhythm appeared almost musical, according to one eyewitness. A psychic who happened to be in the group claimed that a spirit had given her a special show.

THE GOVERNOR'S MANSION IN 1868

WHO'S THERE?

On one occasion several of the tour guides were sitting in the kitchen when they heard and saw a locked door open and shut. The door, which opens to the mansion's offices and lower entrance, is always kept locked to prevent visitors from entering unannounced; only a few people have keys. Their view was blocked by the door, but they clearly heard the click, click, click of high heels ringing down the long, tiled hallway to the stairs. The sound did not continue on up the stairs or around the lower level reception area to the kitchen—it simply died away. One of the guides immediately blocked the two doors on the lower level to prevent an escape, and the others searched the entire mansion, even the closets and cupboards of the private upper level. But they never found anyone to match those footsteps. The mansion was completely empty except for them.

WHERE THERE'S SMOKE ...

In October 1994, during a living history at the mansion, the recently exhumed remains of Confederate captain Ike Turner lay in state for two days, high honor for a Texas soldier whose body was at last being returned home. On this solemn occasion people entered and left the mansion in great numbers. The doorbell rang incessantly, and the front door opened and closed constantly all day long for both days with all the comings and goings—far more activity than was usual.

When the festivities ended and the crowds had finally dispersed, the smell of burned potatoes permeated the lower level, in the room that was once Molly's. The smell was so strong that the staff wondered if maybe the wires had become too hot and caught fire in a wall. The fire department was called, and although all of the firemen smelled the odor, a thorough inspection turned up nothing that might have caused the smell. The staff finally agreed that Molly must have been distracted by the crowds and being too busy to watch her potatoes had let them burn.

One evening in 1994, Krista Kugaraj, a Georgia College student who had helped a caterer serve an elegant dinner at the mansion, was alone in the ballroom mopping the floor. The sudden appearance of a lovely woman startled her so much that she dropped her mop. Kugaraj, who had never seen a ghost before, said the lady smiled and nodded her head in apparent response to her greeting.

The woman was dressed in a dark day dress that was of a style popular among the upper class in the 19th century, but without a hoop. Her hair was pulled back into a bun. She stood there for several seconds, as if checking to see that all was well. "She had a very sweet manner about her," Kugaraj said.

Take a step back into time by touring the old governors' mansion in Milledgeville, and who knows—you too may witness one of the mansion's ghosts!

Open Tuesday through Saturday from 10:00 a.m. until 4:00 p.m., and Sunday 2:00 p.m. until 4:00 p.m. Tours occur on the hour. A fee is charged, with special rates for groups. For more information call 912-453-6404, or write The Governor's Mansion, 120 South Clark Street, Milledgeville, GA 31061.

THE HOMESTEAD

BANSHEES

The Homestead was built in 1818 by Peter J. Williams as a gift for his lovely bride, Lucinda Parke of Greensboro, Georgia. For more than a hundred years the family home was the center of social life in Milledgeville, a gathering center for governors, congressmen and other state officials. Having endured the ravages of age, the home has emerged as one of the great examples of timeless southern grace and charm. The present owner is the great-great-granddaughter of Peter J. Williams.

From the earliest days of the mansion, a ghost resembling a little old lady dressed in gray has been seen walking in the boxwood garden just as the sun is setting. The family claims that she is a banshee, a Welsh spirit who appears at the death of a family member, and that she followed them when they emigrated from Wales. During the War Between the States, the banshee appeared at three different garden parties where she was seen by quite a number of people. Shortly after each of her appearances, the family received word that one of their sons had been killed in the war.

Frances Ferguson, Fanny Way's mother, saw the banshee in the 1930s. When she saw the old lady, Frances said that her mother knew that this time her sister had died.

A family friend claims the most recent sighting of the banshee. In the 1960s, she appeared out of nowhere, a little old woman dressed all in gray from head to toe. He saw her emerge from one of the upstairs bedrooms and walk from one room to another before carefully descending the long, wide stairway. She proceeded slowly down the hall to the front door, turned back

A RECENT PHOTO OF THE HOMESTEAD

to look only once, then passed easily through the closed door, strolled down the front steps, down the front walk past the boxwoods and wisteria and didn't stop until she reached Washington Street. There she paused for a moment, turned left and headed directly to the corner of Liberty Street. She didn't look back, but turned left again and moved swiftly and purposefully along the sidewalk as she passed the Homestead and the Baptist church as she made a beeline directly for Memory Hill Cemetery. She disappeared when she reached the cemetery gate and hasn't been seen since. The family friend can't remember if anyone died when the banshee appeared that time because he was very young.

THE GHOST OF "HONEST JACK"

The Williams's eldest daughter, Sue, was a tall, stately redhead, as beautiful as she was headstrong. Before her father died in 1854, Sue married John "Honest Jack" Jones, the son of a justice on the Georgia Supreme Court. Jones served as the secretary of state of Georgia during the War Between the States. When owner Lucinda Williams died in 1869, Sue gathered much of the family assets to herself and refused to relinquish them to her brothers and sisters.

Sue had grown accustomed to lavish parties and elegant dinners during her childhood, so it was only natural that she assume a position at the center of social life in Milledgeville in the 1850s and 1860s. The Homestead continued to be a popular gathering place even after the state capital was moved to Atlanta.

In 1890 Jones became ill and developed a terrible fever. He grew delirious and had to be tied to the bed for his own safety. But during the night he escaped his restraints and jumped out the window to his death, hitting his head on the rocks in the garden below. A psychic who visited the house years afterward claimed to sense a restless spirit in the house. After suffering a severe chill while in the room where Jones jumped, she described the appearance of a tall, thin man who wore a goatee. Family members couldn't figure out who the man was until someone discovered a picture of "Honest Jack" in the basement—in which he wore a goatee! On another occasion Jones's spirit was seen hovering in front of the window in the upstairs bedroom where he suffered his fatal fall.

MISS SUE COMES BACK

Miss Sue, as she was known, became a recluse after her husband's death. She suffered miserably from bouts of insomnia, and was often seen wandering in the gardens late at night, dressed in her white nightgown. When she died, her niece, Frances Williams Ferguson and her husband David, bought the home.

Frances and her family saw the ghost of Miss Sue in the garden. Several neighbors also claimed to have seen her ghostly form still wandering the gardens at midnight and long after, even into the wee hours of the morning. One man was surprised to see her on a moonlit night, walking among the boxwood and wearing a long formal gown with matching satin slippers.

Mrs. Ferguson's children were so frightened of the ghost that she invented a story to ease their fears. She told them that Aunt Sue had sold some land just before she died, that she had buried the gold from the sale in the garden, and that her spirit was trying to tell them where to find it. Then the children, no longer frightened, eagerly awaited the spirit's visits. They were forever disappointed, however, for they were forbidden ever to dig up their grandmother's precious boxwood gardens to search for the treasure.

RECENT SIGHTINGS

The current resident of the Homestead had a most unusual experience on the night he moved into the house in 1969. He fell asleep, but awoke to the sound of loud voices downstairs. He peered out the front bedroom window and was surprised to see ladies and gentlemen coming up the front walkway, which was lighted by torches. The present concrete steps and buttresses on each side of the front steps had disappeared and in their place wooden steps and balustrades could be seen in the flickering torchlight. A horse-drawn carriage stopped in front of the house, and a group of ladies and gentlemen dressed in clothes from the late 1840s stepped out onto the curb. Several ladies dressed in brightly colored satin gowns greeted them warmly.

The resident started downstairs to see what was going on, but when he reached the main landing, he hesitated, wondering if he were intruding. From this spot he could see much of the ground floor, and what he saw was astounding.

The women guests, he noticed, had come into the front hall and were giving their wraps to a servant. All the furniture was pushed back against the wall in the parlor, exposing a huge area of polished floor. There was music from several fiddlers who were playing merrily in a corner. Tables set up in the long hall wore white damask cloths and held a silver bowl of punch and plates of tiny sandwiches and sweets. The light from the candles in the huge silver candelabra danced and flickered with the changing breeze as the ancient front door repeatedly swung opened and then shut, allowing more guests to enter.

As he reached down to tie his dressing robe tighter, he realized that he was dressed formally in a burgundy brocade waistcoat with tails and black striped slacks. A gold watch chain looped casually out of his pocket. Beads of perspiration erupted on his brow. Just at that awkward moment, when he didn't know whether to join the group or flee back to bed, a slender white hand in a black lace glove reached up and took his, while a soft feminine voice said, "Dear, we've been waiting so long for you to come down. Now we can begin the celebration."

The speaker was a tall, thin woman whose strawberry blonde hair curled up at the ends all around her face. She wore the tiniest black hairpiece with turquoise feathers that matched her turquoise ball gown, an elaborate design decorated with black silk fringe.

Much to his surprise, all of the guests came over and greeted him warmly. He was treated as if he were their long-lost friend. The ladies kissed him on the cheek, and the men shook his hand heartily. The music played on late into the night, and the guests danced in the parlor. He stood at the doorway as some of the guests left and watched them get into their waiting carriages. He waved his good-byes with the others.

When nearly everyone had gone, he spotted a little old lady sitting in the corner of the library. She wore a long gray dress with a white lace collar and a gray veil. It occurred to him that no one had spoken to her all evening, so he walked into the library and greeted her. She looked up and stared directly at him. When she seemed to understand that she had his undivided attention, she pointed to a man in a uniform that may have been from the 1840s, who sat across from them. She nodded her head and said to the resident, "You'll never have to worry."

With that the music stopped abruptly, and he woke up. He found himself lying on the sofa in the library, dressed in his pajamas and robe. The festive scene had vanished, and the rooms were as quiet and as dark as a church on a moonless night.

He's never forgotten the scene, but still wonders if it actually happened or if he was sleepwalking. Years later he discovered some old photos that show the original wooden steps and balustrades—they had been removed in the early 1900s. The early pictures depicted exactly the wooden steps, railing, and balustrades that he had seen in his dream, although at the time he had no way of knowing that the wooden steps had ever existed. Were his distant ancestors actually giving him a message?

He says that not too much has happened there lately. Occasionally he hears unidentified footsteps in the upstairs hall, and once pictures fell off the wall in the upstairs bedroom without any breakage of glass and without the nail falling. Otherwise the house remains peaceful and quiet.

The Homestead is a private residence, not open to the public.

THE TATE HOUSE

Mary Barbara Tate, the current owner of the c.1828 home she named Random House, wonders if the footsteps she hears walking in the front hall belong to the famous ghost of a former owner, Sam Walker, once mayor of Milledgeville.

Walker bought the house in 1870 and lived there with Molly, his third wife; her niece, Alice Dillard; and Joe, his second son by his first wife. There are many local tales of Sam Walker verbally abusing and beating his four wives, even causing their deaths. Louis Andrews, a Milledgeville historian, said Sam Walker appears to have accumulated his fortune by marrying women who were well off; each wife added a plantation to Walker's holdings. Katherine Scott, who owned the house for seventy-five years after Walker died, often said, "The only things Sam Walker loved in his life were roses, Molly and his wife's niece, Alice." He had a marble monument erected on their graves almost as large as his own.

MISS SCOTT'S STORIES

For many years Miss Scott told scary stories all over Georgia about Sam Walker's ghost, making him quite famous. She often told Mrs. Tate stories about the house being haunted by "the meanest man in Georgia."

An article in *Georgia* magazine in October 1973 quoted Miss Scott as saying that "Sam Walker did away with at least three of his wives and was responsible for the deaths of some of his farm help. His first marriage was to a lady in Eatonton. The Negroes who worked for him swore he killed her, but he was never officially accused of anything."

A WROUGHT IRON GATE WITH YELLOW ROSES DECORATES A SIDE
ENTRANCE.

Miss Scott's mother had a cook named Aunt Dorcas, who had once been Walker's slave. One day he accused Dorcas of stealing a ham, and when she wouldn't admit it, he clamped her arm in a carpenter's vice. The cook said her mangled arm gave her mortal fits every time the weather changed for the rest of her life.

Another story told by Miss Scott's mother involved the death of Walker's son, Joe. In 1873, Walker had sent the young man to the Mercer Law School in Macon, hoping they might make a man out of him. There was an epidemic of meningitis at Mercer that year, and the school was closed temporarily. Joe came home immediately, but because Walker didn't want his boy to waste the time in luxury, he sent him across the Oconee River to the Boykin Plantation to replace an overseer who had taken ill. In just a few days Joe returned, saying he felt too sick to work. Walker thought the boy was lying and wanted to send him back to the plantation immediately, but Joe's stepmother insisted that Joe go straight to bed, and she called for the doctor. Walker was furious at her intervention and sent the doctor away, shouting, "The boy isn't ill at all."

On the third day Joe was much worse. He struggled out of bed and staggered to the top of the stairs, hoping to inspire his father to summon the doctor. "Father, I'm dying," he called down in a weak voice.

In response his father shouted, "Nonsense! Get back to bed."

But the effort was too much for Joe, and he fainted, falling headfirst down the stairs and striking his head on each step as he fell. When he landed at the bottom, he was dead. Within the week Molly and Alice had also died of meningitis.

For years Miss Scott claimed to have been frightened by the sound of a heart-stopping thump, thump, thump, in the middle of the night—the sound of a body falling down the stairs. She would get out of bed and search, but she never found the source of the noise. She also claimed to sense an aura of pain in the bedroom where the two women died.

"Sam Walker's nightly ramblings are a replay of the death of his son," she maintained. "The depth of Sam Walker's guilt is so profound that he will tramp these floors until the end of eternity. Or until the house falls down, whichever comes first."

RECENT SIGHTING

Mrs. Tate is intrigued by Miss Scott's stories, but thinks that she may have exaggerated. In any event, she definitely believes her house gives those who live there some interesting and unique experiences.

When Mrs. Tate's sister spent the night in an upstairs bedroom in the early 1980s, she reported hearing a knock, knock, knock at her door. She called, "Come in," repeatedly, but no one replied or opened the door. When Mrs. Tate later denied ever knocking at the door, her sister promptly moved all her belongings downstairs and never returned to the upstairs bedroom again.

And that's neither the first nor the last ghost story. Mrs. Tate and her son were awakened one morning around four o'clock by a thunderous noise in the upstairs middle bedroom. Mrs. Tate ran upstairs but saw no one. Frightened, she and her son sat together downstairs in the living room to wait for the deafening noise to stop. It sounded like bowling balls falling from the ceiling, they reported, and continued unabated until daylight.

On another occasion, Mrs. Tate's son saw the figure of an older woman walking through the kitchen to the sitting room. He thought it was his mother, but later discovered that she had been upstairs, occupied all evening. Mrs. Tate believes it may have been the spirit of her mother, who bought the house from Katherine Scott and died in it.

The front door of the home contains Masonic symbols devised from many varieties of trees that grow naturally in Georgia, assembled on a heavy oaken base in the manner of a parquet floor. Because of its weight, this door is not often used. Family and guests usually enter the house from the side.

Nevertheless, on several occasions Mrs. Tate has heard the sound of the door as it opens and scrapes against the facings, followed by the tap, tap of footsteps entering the hall. Yet the door has never actually opened, nor has anyone ever been discovered in the vicinity when the noises occur.

"These noises are normal, everyday sounds," Mrs. Tate says. She has grown accustomed to them now and simply goes about her daily routine, not knowing nor really caring what the source of the phenomenon is.

The house is privately owned, but the Trolley Tour conducted by the Milledgeville Bureau of Tourism and Trade on Tuesday and Friday at 10:00 a.m., tells many of the stories associated with the Tate House. For more information call 912-452-4687.

MAJOR EDWARD WHITE HOUSE

The Major Edward White House is said to be the oldest house in Milledgeville, dating to about 1806. The two-story, clapboard house built in the plantation plain style boasts a colorful past. Major White was a Revolutionary War hero who lived here when the legislature was in session.

From the 1820s to the 1860s the house was the home and office of Maj. White's son, Dr. Benjamin Aspinwall White. Dr. White studied at Harvard and the University of Pennsylvania and was a very skillful physician who served actively during the Civil War. Over the years many babies were born in his office and presumably several people died there.

Dr. White's son, Samuel Gore White, was also a physician. Samuel's second wife, Catherine, was a native of Milford, Connecticut. Before the war she was the governess for his children, but when the war began she returned home to the North. Singled out as a Southern sympathizer, she was imprisoned for several months. After the war, when Samuel's first wife died, he called upon Catherine to come back to tend his children. He fell in love with the lovely, gentle lady, and they eventually married. Catherine's obituary states that after twenty-seven years as a resident of the South, she had completely adopted it as her home.

In 1866 Dr. Benjamin White supposedly told Samuel that when he died he would give some visible sign that the soul lived on after the heart ceased to beat. Samuel was present at his father's death, and held his father's wrist until the last beat of his pulse faded, but there is no record that he received a sign of any kind. In 1886 the widow of the major's grandson, Edward White II, sold the home out of the family.

MAJ. WHITE'S HOUSE AS IT IS SEEN TODAY

RECENT HAPPENINGS

Paul Campbell, the current owner of the house, has had some unusual experiences there. Campbell has collected some of the books that belonged to both of the doctors White and has restored them to their original home. He has classified them and shelved them in a specific order, but much to his surprise he sometimes finds that they have changed order on the shelves, as if someone had taken them out and then replaced them haphazardly. Occasionally they disappear altogether for a period of time, then mysteriously reappear.

Once in a while he hears footsteps going up and down the stairs, and sometimes the footsteps walk around a discolored area on the floor where a bed once stood.

Campbell says that neither he nor his wife are ever scared. "I guess it just goes with the territory of owning an old house," he says.

In the 1960s and 1970s the house was divided into apartment units, and for a part of that time it was home to a murderer. Sometime in the 1970s the police arrested a man who lived in one of the upstairs apartments. He was convicted of murder, but no evidence was found to prove that a murder ever took place there.

The house is not open to the public, but it is included on the Trolley Tour conducted by the Milledgeville Bureau of Tourism and Trade, Tuesday and Friday at 10:00 a.m. For more information contact them at 200 W. Hancock Street, Milledgeville, GA 31061, or call 912-453-4687.

THE OLD STATE CAPITOL

The 1807 military building that was once the capitol of Georgia is the oldest public Gothic-style building in the United States, although parts have burned down and been rebuilt three times on the same location. The building served as the seat of state government from 1807 to 1868.

Georgia's secession convention was held in its chambers in 1861. An account from a 1936 publication, A Treasure Album of Milledgeville, states:

> In this old building historians agree that the ablest body
> of men ever gathered together in Georgia met on the 16th
> day of January, 1861, in the secession convention. The eyes
> of the nation were turned on Milledgeville at that time, for
> it was believed that the stand that Georgia took upon the
> question of secession would be decisive. Already four states
> had severed the bond of the Union: South Carolina,
> Mississippi, Florida and Alabama.

The secession act was passed on January 19, 1861, and signed on Monday, January 21, with six men writing above their signatures an explanation that they had signed as a pledge to stand behind their state in her hour of need. Little did these men know that in less than four years Georgia would be in flames, with the capitol itself burning brightly.

Yankee general William T. Sherman seized and burned all the Georgia government records up to 1864, and his men even burned the vast state library, throwing all of the leather-bound volumes into a flaming pyre in the moat of the capitol building.

From 1871 to 1880 the building served as the Baldwin County Court House. In 1880 it was converted into a school of higher learning—the

THE OLD GEORGIA CAPITOL BUILDING AS IT LOOKS TODAY

Middle Georgia Military and Agricultural College—as part of the state university system. Now the building is used by the Georgia Military College for administrative offices.

TRAMP, TRAMP, TRAMP

On dark, dark nights, when all the world seems as silent as a tomb, some people have heard the sounds of infantry marching across the green, where the state militia once drilled and performed field marches. On one occasion, in the 1820s, the militia marched relentlessly while the legislature was in session to protest their lack of pay. The state treasury was nearly empty at that time, but the militia refused to wait. Could the sounds be those of the protesting soldiers, still seeking their pay? Or might it be Sherman's army, who marched up Greene Street when they seized control of Georgia?

A Confederate sentry has been seen marching from the gate of the old state capitol and down Greene Street, all the way to the governor's mansion and back again.

Some claim to have heard the sounds of footsteps following them in the capitol legislative chambers, but when they turn around, no one is ever there.

I HEARD A LONESOME WHISTLE CALL

Sometimes, when the wind is just right, the students at Vinson Hall claim to hear the high-pitched sound of a flute or trumpet playing. Could this be the echoes of a long-gone bugler who once sounded taps as the flags were lowered every evening at dusk directly outside their dorm?

The old capitol stands on a knoll of ground higher than the other nearby buildings. When the wind blows through the towers, eerie sounds shrill around the windowpanes. The students call it the "soul winds." Some say the vibrations sound like a person moaning and crying; others say it is more like the howling of wolves.

The State Capitol is included on the Trolley Tour conducted by the Milledgeville Convention and Visitors' Bureau on Tuesday and Friday at 10:00 a.m. For more information call 912-453-4687.

Georgia Military College will also host tours through their museum when renovation of the Old State Capitol Building is completed, possibly in 1997. Write to them at 210 E. Greene St., Milledgeville, GA 31061, or phone 912-454-2700.

THE SPIRIT OF THE BURIAL MOUNDS

In the 1700s, Creek, Hitchiti and Cherokee traders, all part of the great Muskhogean Confederacy, met and exchanged their goods about four miles south of Milledgeville on the Oconee River, in an area that was called Oconee Town. The Cherokees, native to northern Georgia, brought furs, corn, gold and copper. The Hitchiti, who are thought to date back to the pre-Columbian era, brought shells and dried fish from the ocean. The Creeks bartered with clay pots, baskets, grains and other produce.

Oconee Town was a neutral place, where war was declared but not fought and peace treaties were negotiated. It was also the site of special ceremonies, including burials.

A century later, Georgia's Central State Hospital for the Mentally Insane, founded in 1842, was built at Oconee Town. Some say the hospital was built over some of the once-impressive burial mounds that now have all but disappeared, their contents passing undetected by modern civilization.

Sometimes the spirit of a Native American chieftain appears to the staff at the hospital. He is usually seen walking the halls of the fourth floor of the Powell Building. Who he is—what tribe he belongs to and what this restless spirit seeks—no one knows.

Only the elusive chieftain reminds us of the vibrant life that once flourished beneath modern man's mounds of brick and mortar.

The hospital is not open to the public.

MEMORY HILL CEMETERY

Memory Hill Cemetery, a twenty-acre parcel that was designated as a cemetery in 1803 was once one of four public squares in Milledgeville. Many people associated with Milledgeville and Georgia history are buried there, including author Flannery O'Conner and United States congressman Carl Vinson.

For more than thirty years Louis H. Andrews has been the unofficial historian of the cemetery. His own remarkable memory enables him to recall some dark secrets of those who are buried there.

WILLIAM FISH

He recalls William Fish, who lived in Hardwick, just outside Milledgeville. In 1872, Fish's wife and daughter died of typhoid. He was despondent over the tragic deaths of his loved ones and built a brick mausoleum to protect their remains, but these efforts were not enough to console him in his grief.

When the mausoleum was finished, he placed his own comfortable rocking chair inside the small brick building, closed the iron door, sat down in the rocking chair, and shot himself. Now all three skeletons lie side by side for all eternity.

When visitors come to the cemetery, Mr. Andrews suggests that they knock on the door. Sometimes, he says, there is a faint answering knock from the other side.

THE FISH FAMILY CRYPT

THE WITCH

Mr. Andrews tells of a witch who was buried in Memory Hill Cemetery sometime in the 1920s. Legend has it that "she put a curse on everything in sight before she died," he says. The legend also says that should anyone stand between her grave and the witch who inhabits the sun, he or she will be cursed for life.

Dixie Haygood, the woman accused of being a witch, was born in Milledgeville in 1861 and apparently possessed amazing supernatural powers. She was an epileptic, and during her spells she exhibited superhuman strength.

The Milledgeville *Union Recorder* of October 29-31, 1994, reported:

> In her performances she could cause a piano to move
> about the room and chairs to rise from the floor. She could
> find lost objects for members of the audience at random.
> Five men were unable to lift her from the floor, despite her
> small size.

> Dixie performed in front of royalty, including the czar

of Russia, who gave her an emerald. In a London performance, Queen Victoria is said to have swooned. The Queen later asked Haygood to find a missing pearl, said Dixie's great-granddaughter-in-law, Colleen Dubbs of Hobson, Montana.

"The Queen came to Dixie and asked if she could find it. Dixie told her the location and the Queen found the pearl in the exact spot," said Dubbs.

Dixie was able to pick up a table holding several men, and at other times she commanded furniture to leave the room. An amazed audience watched as one by one, each chair or table slid behind the curtain. No visible means was propelling them. She performed for the president of the United States and the governor of Georgia during her long career.

In her book *The Beautiful Side of Evil,* Johanna Michaelsen reports that "Dixie would place her hands upon a chair and without clenching it raise it from the floor. A dozen men were unable to break her hold without twisting or jerking it. Nor were they able to lower a billiard cue held between her fingers or raise it from the floor when she placed it there. She would lay her hands on a raised umbrella and the cover would suddenly rip off."

Eventually Dixie went crazy, reports say, and was a patient at Central State Hospital for the Mentally Insane when she died. She was buried beside her husband at Memory Hill Cemetery.

According to Louis Andrews, it seems that Dixie Haygood, still up to her old tricks, has been playing games or feuding with the Yates family, who are buried next to her.

For the past century a sinkhole has appeared in the Yates's plot every year just before Christmas. Old Mr. Yates's tombstone and that of his daughter just sink out of sight. Andrews blames it on the winter rains. For the past thirty years city workers have filled the hole with cement, gravel, or stone, but each winter the hole reappears.

Could it be the supernatural powers of the witch Dixie Haygood, buried

LOUIS ANDREWS POINTS OUT THE HOLE THAT FORMS UNDER MR.
YATE'S TOMBSTONE. IS IT A WITCH'S TRICK?

in her unmarked grave? Perhaps Mr. Yates seeks to escape her powers. Or perhaps Dixie just wants him moved. Whatever the reason, the mystery remains unsolved.

THE DEVIL'S GATE

Another interesting gravesite in the historic cemetery is protected by a wrought-iron fence that carries the grinning faces of hundreds of little devils. The man who is buried there wanted to be surrounded by the devilish imps for protection from evil spirits in the afterlife.

Only the deceased knows how much protection the imps provide, but

LITTLE IMPS, THOUGHT TO BE PROTECTION FROM EVIL SPIRITS,
DECORATE THIS ELABORATE WROUGHT IRON FENCE.

local legend tells us that on All Hallow's Eve the imps make so much noise that screech owls, alleged to be messengers of death, fill the trees near the gravesite.

Memory Hill Cemetery is generally open daily from dawn to dusk. For information, phone 912-452-3024 or contact Moores Funeral Home, 301 S. Wayne Street, Milledgeville, GA 31061.

GEORGIA COLLEGE

Georgia College was founded as a college for women in 1889 in Milledgeville. Sometime in the 1950s a young woman committed suicide on the third floor of the Sanford Hall dormitory. In the years before the sexual revolution of the 1960s, a pregnancy out of wedlock ruined a woman's reputation forever. It was speculated that the young woman was pregnant and that the fear of telling her parents, being expelled from school and having her reputation tarnished forever was too much for her to bear. Desperation apparently drove her to slit her wrists.

After the tragic death, students who lived in Sanford Hall swore that her spirit haunted the building. Some reported icy cold areas near the end of the hall where the tragedy occurred, and others experienced eerie, uncomfortable feelings when visiting that part of the dorm. Some felt so uncomfortable that they refused to return there.

By the mid-1970s, the area no longer housed any students, serving rather as a gathering place for sororities and fraternities. The suicide tales added extra spice to Halloween parties held there. When asbestos was found on the third floor in the late 1970s, the building was boarded up and remains permanently closed to the public, effectively cutting off but not silencing years of rumor and speculation about the incident and the haunting.

GHOSTS IN RUSSELL AUDITORIUM

Strange events have been known to occur in the Russell Auditorium, built in 1926 on the site of the original Milledgeville Penitentiary and literally atop the ashes of another Georgia College building. The inmates

GEORGIA COLLEGE

burned the prison in 1864 when Sherman's army entered town. Some prisoners escaped while others died in the fire. Ironically, the second building erected there met the same fate, completely burning to the ground. The college had needed an auditorium for years; suddenly they had the resources to build one.

The auditorium brought culture to Georgia College and the people of Milledgeville and has been a great asset to the community. Over the years, many famous people have performed on its stage. Carl Sandberg, Count von Lucker (Germany's famous Sea Devil from the first world war), Flannery O'Conner, Terry Kay and many others have drawn welcoming crowds to hear them speak and perform. Plays, poetry readings, and even the silent films of Douglas Fairbanks, Sr., and Mary Pickford have entertained the audiences.

Not so entertaining are the antics of the ghost or poltergeist that some say inhabits the building. Many people have experienced the inexplicable events that sustain the stories of a mischievous spirit at work. Various stage crews over the years have reported equipment missing—hammers, nails, saws and screwdrivers have disappeared at the most inconvenient times. The workers have searched the entire stage for a missing tool to no avail, only to have it reappear in their toolbox several hours later or even the next day. Or it might be found in a remote location on the far side of the stage.

One time a stagehand standing next to the music pit lost his balance for a second. He caught himself and jumped down safely, but reports that he felt a hand push him off the stage and wonders from where that push came.

Occasionally the stage lights die unexpectedly. Several times they have blinked off in the middle of a performance, forcing the stage crew to light the stage with the glaringly bright house lights. In one case the director liked the scene so much without stage lights that he incorporated the blackout in the play.

Each time a blackout occurs, the college engineer has the wiring checked, but the electrician claims that there is no problem with the wires so far as he can see. They have been updated and are a modern addition to the auditorium. The cause of the blackouts remains a mystery.

In the late seventies the auditorium hosted a performance of a popular play, *Felix the Cat*. Several times during the play a sleek black cat strolled across the stage, always at a most appropriate time. After the performance the crew searched the auditorium for the feline walk-on, but it had disappeared.

Various stage crews over the years have complained of these strange happenings. No one person has ever been identified as the perpetrator. But many people agree that there is a ghost in the Russell Auditorium. When you're in there alone, be alert—maybe you'll hear the sound of a cat or see the dimming of the lights.

Russell Auditorium is generally open for visiting through a backstage entrance, as well as during performances.

ANN SIMPSON SMITH HOUSE

The Ann Simpson Smith House at Georgia College, built about 1947, was named in honor of a distinguished professor of home economics who taught at the college from 1924 to 1969. The two-story brick house once functioned as a model home to give students practical experience in the art of serving tea and other household duties. Home economics lost its appeal as a major focus of woman's education in the 1980s, and in 1987 the college phased out the department.

The Smith House served as a guest house for new professors, visiting speakers and dignitaries, and then as a dormitory until October of 1994.

RECENT SIGHTINGS

In 1994 the new administrative director lived on the first floor of the house for six weeks. She claims that every morning around two or three a.m. she was awakened by the sounds of dishes clanking in the kitchen, which was just across the hall from her bedroom. She heard water running and the sound of footsteps on the linoleum floor, and also thought she heard people laughing in muffled tones amid sudden sounds of exclamation and mumbled chatter, but she couldn't make out any of the words. Most sounds were of a gentle nature, she reports, as if young ladies were making dinner or cleaning up from a tea. On only one occasion was she actually frightened by the sounds. Yet each time she went to the kitchen to see who was making the noise, the noises stopped. The house was as quiet as if the commotion had never happened.

Other guests have heard similar sounds. A family who stayed on the

THE ANN SIMPSON SMITH HOUSE AS IT LOOKS TODAY

ground floor of the house claims to have had trouble sleeping because some noisy students were having a party upstairs during the night. But on that particular night the same director who heard the sounds downstairs slept undisturbed on the second floor. There were no noises.

One of the students who stayed there claims to have heard similar sounds of people talking, but he, too, never discovered the source of the noise.

The director comments that once she admitted the story of the ghosts' social activities to other people, the sounds stopped. "I guess they were mad at me," she says.

Whether or not the spirits were responsible for closing the house to overnight guests is debatable, but college officials claimed to need the house for other purposes. It now houses the college health and fitness center.

A part of Georgia College, the Ann Simpson Smith House is not open to the public.

THE HOUSE ON WILKINSON STREET

In 1995 three coeds at Georgia College rented an off-campus apartment in what appeared to be a solid brick home built about forty years ago. None of the women believed in ghosts or the supernatural at the time, nor were there any known reports of prior ghostly activity there, but as soon as they moved in, strange things began to happen.

One afternoon they found water running from a kitchen faucet, filling the sink, although none of them had turned it on. When they tried to turn it off, the water continued to run as forcefully as if they'd never touched it. And then, strangely, it stopped—just as suddenly as it had begun.

Soon after the water episode, the women began to miss items from the kitchen. First the cheese grater disappeared, and then the cutting board vanished, never to be found. They assumed that a prankster had taken them, but other mysterious things happened that roused their suspicions.

On one occasion, when they were entertaining their boyfriends, the spice rack fell off the kitchen wall, landing right in the spaghetti and ruining their supper. The rack had been attached securely to the wall, but it looked as if the fasteners had been completely pulled out.

One coed swears that whenever her boyfriend visited the apartment the ghostly activity increased. They'd hear unusual noises, and sometimes pictures fell from the wall. Sometimes they felt as if they were being watched. In a back room, when all else was quiet, they could hear someone breathing, and from time to time they'd hear mumbled conversations when they were certain no one else was in the house.

At first the girls thought they might be imagining the strange events, but when each of them experienced the same phenomena on separate

THE HOUSE ON WILKINSON STREET

occasions, they decided that the house certainly was haunted. After a while they grew accustomed to the oddities and simply lived with the spirit.

This is a private home. It is not open to the public.

THE OLD STATE PRISON

The old Milledgeville State Prison, a sinister brick building built in 1911, was the site of approximately 176 executions between 1924 and 1937. Like the notches on the handle of a gunslinger's gun, deep gashes that marked each execution can still be seen in the window sash next to the spot where the original electric chair once stood.

Leo M. Frank, the Jewish owner of a pencil factory in Atlanta, is probably the most infamous prisoner incarcerated at the prison. He was accused of brutally murdering Mary Phagan, a young girl who worked in the factory. He was convicted and sentenced, but was kidnapped by a gang of vigilantes, taken back to Atlanta and mercilessly hanged. In a tragic and ironic turn of fate, Frank's name was cleared of the murder charge seventy years later by an eyewitness who was afraid to come forward at the trial.

Bill Miner, also known as the Gray Fox, was another famous prisoner. His motto was "Have gun will travel," long before the fictional cowboy avenger Paladin had it engraved on his calling cards. Miner ran with such famous outlaw gangs as the Youngers, Daltons, and Jameses. He lived out the end of his life in the state prison, where he died of old age. He is buried in Memory Hill Cemetery in Milledgeville.

During World War II, the building was used by the Naval Ordnance Lab for its headquarters, and it now serves the Forstmann & Co. as a warehouse. Many of the workmen are reluctant to enter the prison to fetch the supplies stored there, but none of them will say why.

The prison has every reason to give rise to frightening tales of ghosts and the supernatural, but no one has ever publicly admitted encountering a ghost there. Nevertheless, the supernatural has a way of expressing itself.

ONLY THE CRUCIFIXION REMAINS OF ONCE EXTENSIVE MURALS IN
THE OLD MILLEDGEVILLE PRISON.

Between 1923 and 1926 large murals depicting scenes from the Bible
were painted on the plaster walls of the dining hall and other rooms by a
French prisoner named Dr. Leon Pons. After more than seventy years of
abuse and neglect, most of the murals have deteriorated so badly that it is
impossible to identify the original subject. All, that is, except the scene that
shows the Crucifixion.

Although the crumbling plaster of the surrounding walls has suffered
extensive damage, the Crucifixion has tenaciously remained, protected by
some mysterious grace to bear witness to the hope of eternal life offered to
the indigent and spiritually infirm. It endures to this day, hidden away on a
dark wall in the original dining hall, a beacon of light to lost souls, whomever
they may be, and a lasting reminder of the power of the supernatural.

Ghosts in the Modern Prison

While the ghosts at the old prison remain quiet, or at least unreported, the situation at the modern prisons in Milledgeville is quite different. Psychiatrists and psychologists occasionally treat prisoners who are haunted by ghosts from their past—and the hauntings aren't always just emotional. Some inmates claim to have been visited by the spirit of a deceased parent or even that of their murdered victims, most often appearing on the anniversary of their death. One unusual report includes visits by a vision of a living person with whom the inmate had unresolved conflicts, a co-defendant in another prison facility.

When prisoners begin talking about ghosts, mental health consultants are called in for therapy. The hallucinatory experiences are as common among non-psychiatric patients as they are among the psychiatric. Extensive trauma histories are typical of those who describe such sightings. A common opinion among the therapists is that the sightings result from stress or flashbacks. Clients are reassured that the visits are harmless.

One psychologist reported that the prison "is the most haunted place I've ever encountered." He thought a moment and then corrected himself. "The prison has the largest concentration of haunted individuals I have ever encountered."

Perhaps there are two kinds of ghosts: those who inhabit the physical landscape—buildings, places, objects—and those who inhabit the internal landscape of the mind. The latter may be more common than we are willing to admit.

The prison is not open to casual visitors.

CULVER KIDD'S DRUGSTORE

Culver Kidd, a distinguished local politician, faithfully served the people of Milledgeville and Georgia as their state representative and senator for almost half a century. From 1948, when he was elected to the Georgia state house of representatives, where he served for twelve years, to 1992, when he retired from the state senate after thirty years of service, Senator Kidd fought effectively for the rights of his constituents. Many improvements in Georgia are the result of his influence, including highway and bridge construction, reforms at Central State Hospital for the Mentally Insane and the establishment of the Culver Kidd Medical facility there, and the creation of thousands of jobs for people in rural middle Georgia.

Born and reared in Milledgeville, Senator Kidd has maintained an office for more than fifty years in the 1890s landmark building on the corner of Wayne and Hancock streets where his father and grandfather, both pharmacists, operated the Culver Kidd Drug Company. For years the building sported a huge round sign that hung over the doorway and boasted: "One minute toothache drops sold for 15¢."

One morning in 1926, around 2:00 a.m., Senator Kidd's father received a call that the drugstore was on fire. When the Kidds arrived on the scene, they discovered it was actually the Elk's building next door that was engulfed in flames. Apparently a waiter who was ironing tablecloths in the basement had left the iron on when he went home. It overheated and caused the fire.

The fire was raging out of control, and the Kidds were afraid the three-story building would collapse on top of their two-story store, so they carried as much merchandise to safety as they could. A woman who was helping them was hit by a falling beam and at first was thought to be seriously

THE TRAIN THAT ONCE PASSED THROUGH MILLEDGEVILLE RAN
RIGHT PAST THE CULVER KIDD DRUGSTORE, SEEN AT LEFT.

injured. But at the hospital a nurse discovered that the "wounds" were merely the orange-red stains of mercurochrome that had splashed upon her when the beam smashed the mercurochrome bottles. Despite the good news, the woman fainted from the shock of the experience.

Senator Kidd remembers that a man was trapped on the second floor of the Elk's building during the fire. He was standing at a window when the back wall of the building collapsed, and the force of wind created by the crashing wall sent him flying. He might have died except that his fall was broken by the awning that shaded the first floor windows.

Another casualty of the fire, a Mr. J. R. Smith, had for many years rented space above the drugstore, where he operated a small tailoring business. He was badly shaken when his rooms were damaged by the fire. The Kidds repaired the damaged roof and painted over the smoke-stained walls, but Smith never fully recovered from the event. One day not long after the fire he was found dead, apparently the victim of a heart attack.

"From that day until now, the office hasn't been the same," Senator Kidd reports. "The spirit of Mr. Smith haunts his old rooms, and we hear the tailor's footsteps often. First Mr. Smith walks across the room to sit a little in the overstuffed chair, but before long we'll hear him walk back. Of course, no one is ever up there."

Senator Kidd says that many people have heard Mr. Smith mumbling, as if he were talking to customers. Sometimes they hear great bumps and long scraping sounds that sound as if furniture is moving around the room. If someone goes up there and moves the file cabinets and chairs to another location, Smith apparently doesn't like it. In no time at all he can be heard sliding the furniture right back to where it was.

Once the maid went to the upstairs office to clean, but she was so scared by Mr. Smith's noisy spirit that she actually jumped the fourteen steps in one leap to get away from him. She swore she'd never return, and she never did.

Senator Kidd and his secretary, Mrs. Reba Webb, have become accustomed to Mr. Smith's noises over the years and leave the upstairs offices to him.

Senator Kidd's offices, once used as the drugstore, are not open to the public.

THE GHOST OF MARION STEMBRIDGE

Even today, more than forty years after his death, the horrible crimes of
Marion Stembridge, whose story was told in *Paris Trout,* a best-selling book
by Pete Dexter later made into a movie, are still discussed among the folks
in Milledgeville. Some say his spirit remains in the building where he once
operated a store and loan office. Others say they have heard his footsteps
in the huge white house on the corner of Columbia and Montgomery streets
that was once his boardinghouse.

Stembridge wore a mantle of respectability as a grocer, but he made his
money as a loan shark of the worst kind—a userer who made loans at
outrageous rates of interest that sometimes took families years to pay off.
His clients were mainly the poor folks in the community who lacked the
credit to borrow money elsewhere, yet over the years he supposedly
accumulated almost a million dollars by squeezing hard-earned pennies
from the most needy of his neighbors.

Stembridge had a history of mental instability and eccentric behavior.
His mother was forced to admit him to Central State Hospital for the insane
several times, and according to local gossip his wife was a wife in name only.
She taught math at Georgia College, and some say he married her so she
could keep his accounts, although others wonder about that, because
Stembridge was a walking adding machine who could add a column of figures
in his head in no time flat and never make a mistake. He supposedly left her
on their wedding night and moved to the Baldwin Hotel when, at the
moment of reckoning, he realized that he was truly a loner. In settlement,
he gave the boardinghouse to his wife.

Whatever the true story, he nevertheless moved into the Baldwin

MARION STEMBRIDGE'S STORE

Hotel, where he rented the entire top floor. He had the locks replaced with heavier, more substantial hardware on all the doors and windows, and he kept the only set of keys.

GETTING AWAY WITH MURDER

One day in 1949 Johnny Cooper decided that he'd had enough of Stembridge's exorbitant interest rates. He brought back the sleek, black sedan that he'd impulsively bought months prior, and dropped it off at Stembridge's store with a message: "You can have this pile of steel in exchange for my note."

The 61-year-old Stembridge was enraged by Cooper's act. He grabbed his .38-caliber revolver and headed toward the shantytown where Cooper lived. "I'm gonna get my money," he said under his breath. "No one's ever gonna treat me like this again." He took with him Sam Terry, one of his employees, as a witness on his behalf, just in case there might be any questions later on.

He roared into the shantytown in a cloud of dust and suddenly slammed on the brakes. "There he is!" he shouted, pointing to his client, who ran up on the porch of a dilapidated one-room house. Stembridge and Terry jumped out of the car and grabbed Cooper by his shirt. They didn't ask any questions, but simply set to beating their helpless victim into a bloody pulp with their brass knuckles.

Two women ran out of the house and yelled at the men to leave their friend alone, but Stembridge and Terry kept on punching. Cooper's face was by now almost unrecognizable. The women tried to pry the men off their victim, but Stembridge flailed about with his brass knuckles, sending one woman flying, then drew his .38 and shot wildly, like a madman, critically wounding both women.

Their anger apparently vented, Stembridge and Terry jumped into their car and pulled away, wheels spinning, hardheartedly abandoning the women who lay bleeding to death on the ground. They never looked back.

Later, desperate for their lives, the two men concocted a story that justified the crime in their own minds and hoped that the fabrication would be accepted by the authorities. Terry said, "Cooper cursed at us, and one of the women pulled out a pistol."

Stembridge said, "It was plainly self defense . . . we had no other choice"—but no one ever found a weapon on the victims.

When one of the women, Emma Johnekin, died in the Richard Binion Clinic, Marion Stembridge and Sam Terry were indicted for murder.

On July 22, 1949, Stembridge was sentenced to serve from one to three years in prison, enough to appease the law-abiding citizens who expected justice, but certainly a light sentence in view of the serious nature of the crime. But Stembridge, thinking that he shouldn't have to serve any time for what seemed to him to be a justifiable action, appealed. He was allowed to go free on bond, pending the second trial.

Stembridge hired three attorneys. One was Marion Ennis, a young,

rising lawyer who was Baldwin County's district attorney, clerk of the
Baldwin County Commission of Roads and Revenues, and a state senator.
The other two were Frank Evans and Jimmy Watts. Ennis wasn't
comfortable with the case, and since he was the county's district attorney,
he withdrew and let the other attorneys take over.

The appeal lasted two days. The ballistics reports proved without a doubt
that a bullet from Stembridge's gun had killed Emma Johnekin. A
twelve-man jury deliberated for twenty-three hours, and their verdict of
"guilty of manslaughter" was unanimous. But Stembridge didn't give up.

Three years later, after two appeals—one to the Georgia courts and
another to the United States Supreme Court—Stembridge was acquitted
on a writ of *habeas corpus*. The courts held that he had been convicted by
prejudiced testimony, and he was a free man. Sam Terry, his accomplice,
was acquitted in a separate trial. Neither man ever served time for the
murder.

A DAY OF RECKONING

Despite his trials and appeals, Stembridge's personal fortune continued
to grow. He reportedly had seven safes in the cellar of his store in which he
stored his money in small bills, fives and tens, because he felt they were
untraceable. Obsessively, he moved his money from one safe to another,
just to fool any would-be thief. He successfully applied to the state for a
banking charter, calling himself the Stembridge Banking Co. He invested
in real estate and bought farms in several counties. Stembridge Road, just
outside Milledgeville near the Oconee River, carries his name.

Eventually, Marion Ennis, having become more and more
uncomfortable with the idea that Stembridge hadn't served any time for his
horrendous crime and hoping to set the record straight, was determined
to reopen the manslaughter case. Ennis realized that Stembridge had very
good political connections when he was unable to raise any interest in a

retrial, but he didn't give up. He enlisted the aid of a young Milledgeville attorney, Stephen T. "Pete" Bivins, who apparently had a plan of his own to deliver justice whether or not the manslaughter case was reopened.

Just about this time the Internal Revenue Service became aware that Stembridge hadn't paid any federal income taxes for more than a decade, and one morning two tax agents appeared at Stembridge's door. Stembridge fixed them with his cold-blooded stare. One eyewitness recalled the ferocity of that stare: "He'd look a hole right through you."

Stembridge hesitated ever so slightly, then coolly offered the agents $10,000 to forget the case and look the other way, but this was one situation his money couldn't fix. On Monday, April 28, 1953, Stembridge was convicted of bribery and ordered to appear for sentencing in seven days. Rumors circulated that Bivins had turned Stembridge in to the IRS.

Even while this was going on, Bivins and Ennis continued to work on the old manslaughter case and eventually uncovered evidence of perjury. The perjury charges were pending against Stembridge as he awaited sentencing for bribery.

It appeared that the infamous scoundrel had finally been pushed into a corner. What would he do now? After years of literally getting away with murder, had Stembridge reached his Waterloo?

An air of festivity permeated Milledgeville on the morning of May 3, 1953. In honor of the 150th anniversary of the city's founding as Georgia's state capital, the entire town was festooned in red, white, and blue, and many of the people were dressed in period costume. Parade floats and craft booths were being decorated and excitement ran high in anticipation of the finest celebration ever to be seen in the town.

But that morning Marion Stembridge, deep in the cellar of his store, was not celebrating. He knew that in two days he would be sentenced, and he knew in his bones that the judge would send him to prison. At the same time, he was dead certain that he'd never see the inside of a prison cell. He finished whatever he was doing and whistled as he ascended the steps

THE SANFORD BUILDING, WHERE MARION STEMBRIDGE KILLED
STEPHEN T. "PETE" BIVINS AND TOOK HIS OWN LIFE

into his grocery store, nodding as he passed the clerk, saying that he was going to invite his mother to watch the parade with him.

But instead of going to his mother's home, he went to the office of Marion Ennis above the Campus Theater. He took the steps two by two, and nothing in his step gave anyone cause to think that for Stembridge this was anything other than an ordinary day. Ennis was surprised to see him.

Without a word of warning, Stembridge drew a .38-caliber revolver, which he had hidden beneath his coat, and fired three shots into Ennis's chest and shoulder. The 46-year-old attorney crumpled to the floor, where he died in a widening pool of blood. He left behind a lovely widow and two small children.

The coldhearted Stembridge then walked swiftly down Hancock Street, still whistling as he passed a few ladies out for the festivities. He climbed to the second floor of the Sanford Building, to the office of Pete Bivins. Bivins, apparently expecting his fellow attorney, called out, "Is that you, Ennis?"

Stembridge again pulled out his gun and fired once, hitting the

27-year-old Bivins in the chest. Bivins managed to pull his own gun out of his desk, but he died before he could fire it.

Stembridge then stuck the barrel of his pistol in his mouth and fired. The coroner had to deal with three dead bodies that day.

AFTERMATH

Becky Hodges was two doors down from the theater in the beauty parlor getting her hair styled for the gala to be held that night. She remembers that someone ran into the shop and yelled, "Marion Ennis is dead—someone's just shot him!" The women in the shop screamed. She recalls that part of her hair was up in rollers and the other part down. "Everything stopped dead. Just as dead as those bodies. The next thing I knew—it was only minutes later, we hadn't gotten over the shock of Ennis yet—another person ran in and said two more had been killed, Pete Bivins and Marion Stembridge. It was as if a bomb had fallen. All the parties and festivities were canceled. The food was taken to the funerals. I never got my hair fixed that day."

RECENT SIGHTINGS

The house with "fish-scale shingles" surrounding the second floor that once was Stembridge's boardinghouse is now inhabited by Georgia College students. In Stembridge's day the second floor was divided up into four rooms. His was the one on the left as you face the house from Columbia Street.

A Georgia College student who lived in that room for six months claimed that every couple of nights he'd be awakened at about one or two in the morning by the sound of heavy footsteps walking down the hall. They'd stop at his door, and he'd hear the sound of a key turning in the lock. He could see nothing, but he'd hear his door creak open and the footsteps

MARION STEMBRIDGE'S BOARDINGHOUSE STILL STANDS.

would continue into his room, stopping just short of his bed. The sounds almost drove him crazy until he realized that he had been sleeping in Stembridge's old bedroom. He continued hearing the footsteps, but they didn't bother him anymore.

Stembridge's boardinghouse can be seen at the corner of Montgomery and Columbia streets in Milledgeville, GA. The Sanford building has been torn down.

MACON

THE HAY HOUSE

For the past one hundred twenty years the ornate residence on Georgia Avenue in Macon has been home to the Johnston, Felton and Hay families. Over the years descendants have denied any claim that the mansion is haunted, and the current director and staff deny the house is haunted, but when I asked around Macon, I heard otherwise. Intrigued, I finally decided to see for myself.

One Sunday afternoon in 1993 I toured the mansion to absorb the ambiance of the place and take a few pictures. The house was truly elegant, dressed as it was for a wedding that was to take place that evening. The heavily fluted, walnut stair railing was draped with garlands of evergreens accented with white satin bows and crowned with huge, sweet-smelling magnolias. Some workers were setting up a stand in the ballroom, while another was placing potted palms around the room.

I prepared to take a picture of the dark, arched doorways and the mounted animal heads that hung from the walls, but just as I was about to snap the shutter I saw something out of the corner of my left eye, like the hem of a long skirt, floating in the air above my head. The folds of the skirt were transparent, like huge gathered cobwebs, and appeared very clearly against the dark wood moulding under the stairs. The toes of tiny shoes peeked out from beneath the skirt, and a ghostly woman seemed to be walking toward me—as if she were slowly descending invisible stairs. She paused after each step with the kind of dignity that demands respect. Her demeanor was regal and very commanding.

I tried to take a picture of the ballroom, but the spirit suddenly flattened out and became a screen that blocked my view, then disappeared. I couldn't

THE HAY HOUSE AS IT LOOKS TODAY

forget the grace and dignity that she had displayed. I felt that I'd been in the presence of a great lady, yet I was a little shaken by the experience, because she was the first ghost I'd ever seen. Curiously, after the the spirit faded away, I felt a deep sense of pain, melancholy and even tragedy, which lingered most of the afternoon. I was both greatly disappointed and immensely relieved that she hadn't stayed very long, and hoped that I'd caught some evidence of her on film.

Later, to my great surprise and disappointment, I discovered that the shutter speed had somehow changed from sixty to three—far too wide open to register a gossamer vision. Even though I'd received special permission to take pictures in the mansion, the ghost apparently had disapproved.

I wondered who the spirit might have been. After checking several editions of the old *Macon Telegraph*, it was clear that despite denials from family and staff, I wasn't the first to see the ghost—and probably would not be the last.

THE JOHNSTONS

In 1855 William Butler Johnston, a retired jewelry broker and railroad magnate, began to build the twenty-four room Italian Renaissance villa for his bride, Ann Tracy. The Johnstons fell in love with the foreign architectural style while honeymooning in Italy and imported a vast assortment of building materials that included nineteen rare Carrara marble mantels, twelve-foot-tall hardwood interior doors and the massive front doors.

The home, which took five years to build, was regarded as one of the finest of its kind in the South, even in the nation. It was one of the first in the nation to boast the newest inventions of the day: indoor plumbing with hot and cold running water in its three bathrooms and an extensive ventilation system.

The Johnstons also included among their honeymoon purchases a vast assortment of art treasures. With twelve hundred square feet of floor space and a thirty-foot clerestory ceiling, the picture gallery was one of the most spectacular rooms in the house. They thought so much of a marble statue of the biblical Ruth by the famous sculptor William Randolph Rogers that they built a special room to house it, and decorated it with clouds and stars on the ceiling. The Johnston's granddaughter called it "Ruth's room."

Despite the beautiful home, the Johnstons' family life was filled with tragedy. Their first child, Francis Campbell, was born on August 23, 1852, in Paris, while the couple was still on their grand tour. Unfortunately, the baby died shortly after birth. The shock of the loss caused a decline in Ann Tracy's health, and the Johnstons remained in Europe two years longer than expected. They returned to Macon in 1854, and by 1855 were expecting their second child. Susan Mary was born that August, but died from croup the following spring. Ann Tracy had a third child, William Butler, Jr., who also fell victim to the croup just two months after his birthday. Edward Tracy, their fourth child, was born on February 22, 1860, and also died of croup at two months old.

The couple were so distraught that they delayed finishing the upstairs of the house and spent two lonely years living in the rooms on the basement level. Ann Tracy was often confined to bed with her grief. When she did make an appearance she always wore black, along with two black bands on each arm.

In July 1862, a daughter was born, the Johnstons' fifth child. She was named Caroline in memory of Ann's younger sister, who had just died, leaving motherless her nine-month-old son. Caroline survived to old age, as did the Johnstons' sixth child, Mary Ellen. In addition to her own girls, Ann Tracy reared her sister's son and her deceased brother's two children, so after years of tragedy and heartache, the activities and joyful noises of five healthy children finally filled the house.

DURING THE WAR

The Johnston home was at the center of what passed for the Macon social scene during the war. Many famous and influential people crossed its threshold, including the president of the Confederacy, Jefferson Davis, who dined at the Johnstons' table.

William Johnston served as receiver for the general depository in Macon, which protected the largest share of Confederate gold held outside Richmond. At various times there was as much as $1,500,000 in gold in his care. Some speculate that the treasure may have been stored in a secret room on the third floor landing of the mansion, but others dispute that claim, arguing that the wooden floors couldn't possibly have borne the weight. Still others suggest that the gold may have been kept in a safe hidden in the vast cellars of the mansion.

In any event, when the destitute men of the Macon Militia pleaded their need for food and medicines, Johnston immediately produced $125,000 in gold for their use. No one knows for certain where this money came from, since most of the South's treasury was held in London banks.

During the last days of the Confederacy, Sherman bypassed Macon on his destructive march to the sea, thus saving the grand old homes there from his blazing torches. Refugees and wounded soldiers swarmed into Macon from Atlanta, Milledgeville and surrounding communities, crowding the city beyond its limits.

The war officially ended on April 9, 1865, but Union general James H. Wilson attacked Macon from the south three weeks later. He aimed his cannons and artillery at the cupola of the Johnston mansion, but the huge cannonballs fell short, blasting deep holes in the earth that remained unfilled until several years ago, a reminder of the intended destruction. On May 3, 1865, Governor Brown surrendered the Georgia troops, and the war was over in Macon.

AFTER THE WAR

After the war, the mansion remained the center of Macon society for many years, like a dowager empress among the great estates. The house was passed on to the Johnstons' daughter, Ellen Tracy Felton, and then to her son, William, who finally sold it in 1926 to the Hay family. At that time the Johnstons' extensive art collection was sold and dispersed.

By the 1950s time had taken its toll, and the upkeep and repairs of the mansion proved to be too expensive even for the most affluent. The once great lady declined for a period of time, but Hay endowed a foundation to maintain the home after his death. The mansion, now known as the Hay House, is part of the National Historic Trust, open to the public as a museum.

RECENT SIGHTINGS

In 1980 funds were secured to save the 120-year-old mansion, and the extensive renovations began. A former director of the Hay House, Fran La

Farge, now deceased, was convinced that supernatural activities occurred in the 18,000-square-foot mansion during the renovations. Many of the workmen and staff not only confessed an awareness of unusual noises and movements, but they reported the appearance of apparitions almost daily. Spirits from the past, apparently freed from some unknown entombment, trotted out to take a look at the effects of the hammering, scraping and painting. Though many of the spirits remain nameless, they seem to be mysterious visitors who linger within the massive brick walls, protected from the passage of time as if held in state and preserved in a mausoleum fit for a king.

Mrs. La Farge reported that a maid once saw the figure of a ghostly woman standing in the hallway. She knew what Ann Tracy Johnston looked like from her portrait and other pictures in the house and thought this must be the spirit of the former lady of the house because her hair was braided exactly like Mrs. Johnston's. She was so frightened that she left the upper floors and refused ever to go back alone.

According to her family, Mrs. La Farge experienced another supernatural event late one night when she was alone in the house. She sensed that another person was with her in the dining room and was startled by a sudden blast of hot air, as hot as if she'd opened an oven. Before she could regain her senses, the hot air was immediately followed by a blast of icy cold air. She was frightened by the episode, but tried to brush it off by making light of it.

Not too long afterward, again alone in the house in the evening, Mrs. La Farge heard footsteps on the stairs that lead to the second floor. She was convinced that someone was there and got up to check, but found no one. Moments later the security sensor began clicking away, as if someone were indeed climbing the stairs. That was when she began to believe in ghosts, her family reports.

In 1984 an article entitled "Are There Ghosts in the Hay House?" by Terri K. Smith appeared in the *Macon Telegraph and News*. It describes some of the ghosts seen in the Hay House and quotes Fran La Farge. Part of it is reprinted here with permission.

Chester Davis worked as a houseman and later a tour guide for the Hay House for "two months short" of 29 years. He doesn't believe in ghosts and never saw anything unusual until the renovations began in 1980.

Davis' first experience with an unusual visitor was in the dining room of the big mansion, where he was polishing the silver hardware on the doors. He said he glanced up from his work and saw "a gentleman in his early 50's in the dining room. He had on blue pants, a white shirt and looked like he was about 55 years old. He had on an open collar like mine, and his hair was pepper gray. He had a real nice haircut—it was not a hippy haircut—and it was slightly parted in the center."

The man glanced at Davis "like he wanted to ask me what I was doing," Davis said, but when Davis looked back up, the man had vanished. Davis never said a word about what he had seen. "I didn't say anything because people would think I was crazy," he admitted.

His next visitor appeared at the front door around noon one day. "She was an elderly white lady, looked to be in her 60's, wearing a long, blue and white checked dress," Davis recalled. "She looked like she had been working in the garden. She had on a straw hat with a wide brim, kind of a yellow gold color, like a field hat. She reached for the doorbell, and that's when I got up to see what I could do for her, and she just disappeared."

The next day he said he was polishing the large hinges on the front door, when he looked up and spotted a woman standing on the edge of the lawn near the front driveway to the house. "She might have been in her late 30's, or early 40's, and she was wearing what looked like a netted dress. It was flimsy and on the purple side, kind of light purple, not a deep violet like the flower. She had a hat sitting kinda sideways that matched the dress. She weighed about 120 pounds," Davis remembered. "But when I looked at her for a second time she had disappeared."

Davis never saw any other human apparitions, but he said he did see something rather strange one day. ... "It was in the grand ballroom. I looked up at the ceiling and saw a large black bird. His wings were ... probably four feet long and ten feet wide. He was flying east across the ceiling."

But still Davis said nothing—until he heard the unusual stories of other employees and realized that something strange was indeed going on. Years later, at 75 years of age, he still questioned his own sightings.

An earlier article in the *Macon Telegraph and News,* on May 2, 1981, bore the following headline: "Hay House 'Ghost' Sends Out Messages."

There is a grave matter to discuss these days at the Hay House. And Thursday night, the house director, a local radio personality, his wife and a reporter met with a "sensitive" woman in an attempt to communicate with the spirits that have been reported there.

Since the beginning of April workers at the Hay House have sighted five ghosts and have experienced strange and what one worker calls "evil" feelings in the house," Fran La Farge, director of the Hay House said. "The five sightings include figures of two females, two men and a small child. And these aren't the only strange things that have been reported around the house," Mrs. La Farge said.

"A few people recall feeling something very unpleasant in the house or seeing brilliant lights. Twice, Danielle

D'Assaro, the assistant director of the Hay House, has seen long skirts move behind a door," La Farge said.

Ms. D'Assaro said she and Mrs. La Farge saw a chandelier in the house swinging. "The chandelier was moving back and forth and all the crystals were clanging together." And three times the fire alarm at the house has sounded for no apparent reason. "A thought went through my mind that the ghost had materialized in front of the smoke alarm," she said laughing. She seems to find the strange happenings hard to believe, but she doesn't doubt what others have seen or felt.

Mrs. La Farge said she thinks the ghosts are appearing because of the restoration going on right now [1981] with all the hammering and the scraping. "We're changing the color back to what it was in 1876, and they are either expressing their approval or their disapproval."

Mrs. La Farge asked an automatic writer, a person who produces a script supposedly written by spirits, to visit.

The automatic writer, a Macon woman who will be referred to as Mrs. X, because she didn't want to be identified, began by having the group walk around the house. She said the spirits were there and were "shouting" to her. She said, "They want to talk."

As they walked through the bedrooms on the third floor, Mrs. X said the spirits were following them. Both Mrs. La Farge and the radio announcer said they sensed the spirits were there. The radio announcer's wife, who called herself a skeptic, said she didn't feel anything strange.

When they went down stairs, Mrs. X ... began to meditate, breathing very deeply in the quiet room, which was lit by candles. She sat with a pen resting in her hand

and paper in front of her.

Suddenly, her hand jerked and she began to write. She wrote the name "Anne" in a beautiful script. Anne was the name of the first owner's wife. Mrs. La Farge began to ask questions, and Mrs. X wrote that the restorations are good. "But you must leave the basement."

Later, Mrs. X was again writing from Anne, and she wrote about the basement. "Be careful" and "Very Valuable." But the pen wouldn't answer questions about what the workers should be careful of in the basement. Ms. X wrote "my secret."

Later in the evening when Ms. X was trying to meditate, she said she couldn't because of an overwhelming sadness and a coldness she was feeling five paces behind her.

When she did begin writing she wrote the name "Marshal McAdoo" and the name "visitor." Then she wrote "my love left me—Caroline." Caroline was one of the original owner's daughters. And then she wrote, "I died."

The final message Ms. X wrote was from "Walter." The written message said, "every body is here and they all want to talk," but it read "too much hurry."

Many directors have come and gone since 1981. The current director and her staff deny any and all references to the ghosts, but the evidence is clear that spirits still linger in and around the Hay House.

The Hay House is open to the public for visitors to tour six days a week, Tuesday through Saturday, 10:00 to 5:00 and Sunday 1:00 to 4:30. For more information write The Hay House, 934 Georgia Avenue, Macon, GA 31201 or phone 912-742-8155. A visit to Macon is not complete without seeing "the palace of the South."

THE BEALL HOUSE

Some speculate that one of the ghosts in the Beall house in Macon is the wealthy railroad tycoon, Leonidas A. Jordan. Others yearn to know the identity of the young woman who allegedly jumped to her death from the second-story study window, and what inner tortures might have caused such a desperate act. One thing is certain, however—many restless spirits inhabit the gracious antebellum mansion, now a fine-dining restaurant called Beall's 1860, and occasionally they taunt the employees and visitors alike.

Nathan Beall, a wealthy cotton plantation owner and speculator, built the Georgian style mansion in 1860. He owned two cotton plantations in Georgia, one in Sandersville and one in Hancock County, and a cotton brokerage firm, Dunhill and Beall Co., Inc., in Macon.

THE WAR

The family—Nathan, his wife Martha, son George and daughter Juliet— spent most of their time in their comfortable home in Macon and were living there when the War Between the States was declared and Georgia seceded from the Union.

On July 10, 1861, twenty-year-old Juliet married Dr. George G. Griffin, a young physician with promising prospects. On January 11, 1862, Griffin was appointed an assistant surgeon in the Confederate States Army, and on March 15, 1862, he was ordered to a hospital in Petersburg, Virginia. On February 1, 1863, he was ordered to report for duty in Macon on September 27, 1863. Tragically, he disappeared somewhere between Petersburg and his hometown, never to be seen again.

THE BEALL'S 1860 HOUSE TODAY. THE COLUMNS WERE ADDED
IN THE EARLY 1900s.

His young wife never recovered from the pain of his loss. Legend tells us that Juliet often sat in the study off the second story bedroom in her father's house where she could see the road and watch for his return.

On March 4, 1862, George Beall, who was then eighteen, enlisted as a private in the 47th Regiment of the Georgia Infantry. He was listed present on the roll of February 28, 1863, but he, too, disappeared, never to be heard from again.

Nathan Beall, who had already lost his son and his son-in-law, then lost his plantations and his cotton business to Sherman's torch. In 1865 he sold Beall House to Leonidas A. Jordan, the richest man in Georgia after the war, for what was at the time an exorbitant sum of $30,000. Col. Beall, then a widower, and his daughter moved to a more modest home in Macon. During the Reconstruction, Yankees occupied the house for a short time, but Jordan soon moved in to stay.

AFTER THE WAR

Jordan was a well-loved philanthropist, a financier of the Macon Academy of Music and a founder of the Macon opera. He brought his bride, Julia Hurt Colquitt, well known to Confederate soldiers as "the belle of the South," to the mansion in Macon, where they lived happily together until December 1891.

Julia, who was on a holiday visit to her mother in Columbus, Georgia, was suddenly taken ill with influenza and pneumonia. Word was sent to her husband that she wouldn't be home for Christmas, and in fact, she died on December 30.

After her death, the 68-year-old Jordan fell ill himself, but his vigor increased when he was introduced to a headstrong young woman who vaguely resembled Julia as a young lady. The fascinating debutant was 21-year-old Ilah Dunlap, the daughter of a neighbor. Jordan, who was worth well over a billlion dollars at that point, fell madly in love with her almost instantly and, according to numerous reports, essentially bought Miss Dunlap's affection. Some say real money changed hands. In any event, on April 11, 1893, the childless Jordan signed a new will bequeathing all of his vast international fortune to Miss Dunlap. Two weeks later they were married and set off to tour Europe with the entire Dunlap family.

Jordan's health declined for the next six years, but his new wife refused all visitors. Jordan died in 1899, alone in the house. "Without family or friends nearby," wrote a distraught Martha Gardner, a childhood friend who had been forbidden to see him in his last days.

Miss Dunlap's lack of affection for the man is evidenced by the simple county marker that identifies his grave beside his family's elaborate marble monument to this day. Her marble mausoleum, on the other hand, which carries the name Dunlap, is the largest in Macon's Rose Hill Cemetery. She sold at auction all the family silver engraved with his and Julia's initials as well as many of the furnishings and priceless family heirlooms. She sold the

Beall home itself to her brother in 1902; he was the one who added the Greek Revival columns and veranda.

Ilah Dunlap Jordan spent years vacationing in Europe on her inheritance. She married and returned home for a short time, but then returned to Europe. She died in 1939 in Germany. The family had great difficulty in bringing her remains home because Nazi Germany refused to allow her body to clear customs. It had to be cremated before the authorities would release it.

Ilah endowed the University of Georgia with funds to build the Ilah Dunlap Little Library. Her portrait and furnishings can be seen in the Georgia Room today along with some momentos that belonged to Leonidas Jordan. His name has never been included on any bequest from her estate. To this day few people know the true source of Ilah's largesse.

Perhaps the fury of the multimillion dollar railroad magnate has resisted the grave and lives on, enduring in the form of the poltergeist in the restaurant.

RECENT SIGHTINGS

On Christmas Day in 1993, 102 years after Julia's death, and after the mansion had become a restaurant, the waiters reported that all the pipes in the house shook and trembled for an extended length of time, making an ear-splitting racket. The experience was so profound that they at first thought there had been an earthquake. Although the timing of this incident was very near the anniversary of Julia's death, it wasn't the first such activity to have occurred in the house. Perhaps Jordan's spirit is still mourning the death of his beloved Julia.

But Jordan's spirit apparently is not alone. A former *maitre d'hotel* reported that restless spirits and poltergeists definitely lurk in the old house. After working in the restaurant for five years, he believed the house to be haunted. On his first day of work he was given the task of scrubbing the

THE STAIN THAT WILL NOT GO AWAY MARKS THE SPOT WHERE A

YOUNG WOMAN PLUNGED TO HER DEATH.

concrete porch with a solution of bleach and water to remove a large brown stain directly beneath the study window, the window from which some unfortunate woman jumped to her death.

The stain is about two feet wide and irregular in shape, with spots of the same color scattered around it. When it is bleached the stain disappears temporarily, but after several hours it returns, completely intact. The *maitre d'* has repeated this process hundreds of times. Now he believes his effort is futile.

On one occasion in 1994 the 12th Georgia Brigade of Confederate reenactors, wearing their full-dress uniforms, dined in the upstairs banquet hall. During the dinner the lights on each of the two huge antique brass chandeliers flickered off and on in sequence—first one, then the next and the next—until they were all flickering at various intervals. This would be an impossible feat to accomplish by hand, because both chandeliers are controlled by the same switch and wired to turn on and off simultaneously. The display both dazzled and baffled everyone in the room. They wondered if the prank was caused by the spirit of someone who had lived in the house who might have been a member of the original 12th Georgia Brigade, a unit comprised primarily of Macon men.

On another night, a waiter was fixing drinks in the upstairs bar when the ice cubes began to pop out of the glasses, like popcorn hopping out of a hot pan. He tried to put the cubes back into the glasses, but they continued to pop out in a frightening display. Frantic, he left the room, vowing never to return again.

At that same bar on another busy night, a bartender noticed a young girl dressed in a long white gown sitting quietly on one of the stools. He turned around to get a soda, and when he looked back the girl had disappeared. No one else working that night could remember seeing anyone fitting the girl's description. Could this apparition have been the girl who jumped to her death from the study window? Or could it have been a vision of Jordan's first wife, the beautiful Julia?

On yet another night, when a waiter was preparing for a large party, all of the glasses that had been washed and placed on the bar to dry were swept onto the floor by some mysterious hand and shattered into thousands of pieces. No person was near enough to cause the disaster—the glasses appeared to fly from the counter by themselves. The waiter thought it must have been the poltergeist.

In the restaurant office one evening the manager was totaling up the receipts when he came across one that was dated ten years earlier. It stood out from the rest because the paper had browned slightly from age. He puzzled over it for a few minutes, but thinking that it must have dropped out of a box of old receipts, he crumpled it up and threw it away in the trash. An hour later it mysteriously reappeared on his desk.

Many of the supernatural activities occurring in the house seemed to happen upstairs, in the small room thought to have been Jordan's study. Before the renovations, bookshelves lined the north wall of the room. Sometimes, without warning, all of the books would fly off the shelves and land in a pile in the center of the floor. This happened so often that the management finally removed the book shelves altogether.

On other occasions, a lamp in that room was discovered burning when everyone was sure it had been turned off. The lamp in question is touch-activated—light pressure on the base turns it on or off. Sometimes the gas log in the fireplace burns without anyone lighting it. Maybe Julia made sure that a fire burned there to warm her husband on cold evenings.

A tourist who was busy capturing the lovely interior of the home on videotape was surprised when her camera malfunctioned when she entered the study. She turned it off, thinking that the tape had broken. The next morning when she checked the camera she discovered that it worked just fine.

The *maitre d'* claimed that he has grown accustomed to the strange activities in the Beall's 1860 House. He doesn't believe that the spirits are malicious, just mischievous. One thing is fairly certain—something traumatic must have happened in that tiny room on the second floor, because the spirits have lingered there for years. We will never know the whole truth; all we can do is speculate.

Bealls 1860 restaurant is located at 315 College Street, Macon. For dinner reservations call 912-745-3663. Open Monday through Saturday.

ST. JAMES CHURCH

The vicarage at the eighty-year-old St. James Episcopal Church in Macon had been vacant for fifteen years before Father Robert Gibson and his wife Joy moved in in December of 1975. On their first night in the house Mrs. Gibson was awakened at two-thirty by a noisy clatter in the kitchen; it sounded as if pots and pans were being tossed about the room. She saw what she thought was a flash of light coming from that direction, but when she reached the hallway that led to the kitchen, everything was quiet and dark.

She was puzzled by the noise, but headed back to bed, thinking that the flash of light might have been the headlights of a passing automobile and that the noise might simply be the house settling. But when she reached the bedroom, she heard another loud, sharp crash—as if one last pot had been hurled across the kitchen. She awakened her husband, who had slept through the onslaught. He accompanied her back to the kitchen, and they checked the cupboards but found no reason for the unusual sounds.

On another occasion, not long afterward, some guests who were in the kitchen were surprised when suddenly the cabinet doors began to open and close on their own—first one, then another, and another. Before they knew it, five cabinet doors were swinging wildly back and forth, and then, without warning, they all slammed shut. In another incident footsteps were heard crossing the living room, toward the front door. The door opened and shut by itself, and the footsteps tapped across the porch before they faded out of hearing.

The ghost-poltergeist, named Stella by a parishioner, didn't appear again for some time after the kitchen cabinet incident, but several weeks later the Gibsons were awakened by the sound of their child's toy piano apparently

THE VICARAGE OF ST. JAMES EPISCOPAL CHURCH

playing by itself. This happened twice, both times at two-thirty in the morning, when their children were fast asleep. On another occasion Mrs. Gibson noticed the pungent smell of cheap perfume permeating the room, especially the area surrounding the place where she stood.

One day, as she cut through a building that stands between the vicarage and the church sanctuary and was at the time vacant, she heard the murmur of ladies' voices. It sounded as if they were having tea, but the building was empty and there was no one in the church next door. Perhaps, she thought, Stella and her friends had moved into the vacant building.

One year when the choirs were singing a special Christmas program, the candles in the sanctuary began to flicker to the rhythm of the music.

Another Episcopal priest's car once broke down near the church, and he called to ask if he and his wife could spend the night with the Gibsons. The couple slept on the pull-out couch in the living room, but in the middle of the night they were suddenly awaked by the deafening sounds of baroque organ music booming out at them from the center of the front wall. The barrage continued for about ten minutes, then subsided. Understandably, the couple were reluctant to spend another night in the vicarage.

What caused the noise? That question may never be answered; however, an organ may well have stood against that wall at some time in the eighty-year history of the vicarage.

A mental health clinic eventually rented the vacant building between the vicarage and the sanctuary. On one occasion the staff reported that boiling hot water inexplicably churned and bubbled up in the porcelain toilet bowls. On another occasion a mirror came away from the wall several inches, as if someone were lifting it from its hook, and dropped straight to the floor but didn't break.

Stella's at it again, the Gibsons thought. They hoped that Stella had moved next door permanently, but the clinic staff members were nearly hysterical. At first it was hard for them to understand how the Gibsons could have accepted such antics in their own home so calmly. They eventually got used to the idea of a ghost living in the house when Stella's pranks grew fewer and the times between grew longer.

Eventually the Gibsons moved out of the vicarage and into a condominium. Several subsequent residents of the vicarage have seen Stella's ghostly form on various occasions. They have all treated it lightly, sure that Stella is harmless.

STELLA MOVED, TOO

Shortly after the moving, the Gibsons held a reception for their family and friends to celebrate their daughter's eighth-grade graduation. Father Gibson, his father and his father-in-law each saw a Victorian lamp slide to the edge of the table as if it were being pushed and fall slowly into a chair without breaking. Beads of perspiration broke out on their brows, and they shook in their shoes, Father Gibson reported, but that wasn't the end of the show. A paperweight also slid to the edge of the table and fell into the chair, again as if someone were pushing it. Father Gibson, not knowing what else to do, replaced the glass items on the table and made light of the incident, telling the guests that the demonstration was from their own personal poltergeist.

Shortly thereafter Mrs. Gibson misplaced her reading glasses and was forced to order new ones. Several days later she discovered them in a box wrapped in paper and pushed far under their bed. The glasses were the first large object that they suspected Stella of hiding. She had on other occasions played with the kitchen utensils, messing them up and moving them around, but she had never hidden them away.

A week after the graduation party incident, Mrs. Gibson saw an apparition in their courtyard. An old lady, her hair pulled back into a bun, danced in circles above the spa. She appeared to be sweet and harmless, but Mrs. Gibson felt sure that she now knew who had engineered all the ghostly pranks for the last twenty years.

She thought, "Stella's back," and was surprised at how much she had missed her. Stella's ghostly form was visible for only an instant, then rose into the air for several seconds before disappearing through a neighbor's brick wall. The Gibsons didn't hear her or see Stella again until the following April, when similar pranks occurred.

The Gibsons never knew where Stella came from or who she was, but it seems as if she always made her presence known in the month of April.

The vicarage at St. James is not open to the public.

THE WOODRUFF HOUSE

In 1993, when police sergeant Pat Wood first entered the mansion for her midnight-to-eight shift, an overwhelming feeling of hostility greeted her. She wanted to flee the house immediately, but she couldn't; someone had recently broken in and stolen a priceless antique chandelier, and her job was to protect the house and its contents.

The Woodruff House, a Greek Revival plantation-type mansion with eighteen huge columns across the front, was constructed for Jerry Cowles by master architect Elam Alexander in 1836. Aptly named Overlook when it was built, it crowns the hill above Macon and is visible from a great distance.

Both Cowles and the second owner, Col. Joseph Bond, provided leadership in the early growth of Macon. Cowles, a railroad financier and banker, was the largest contributor in the first subscription of Wesleyan College, and mainly through his efforts "Encampment Hill" was chosen for its location. Joseph Bond was the most influential and successful cotton grower in Georgia; the street on which this heritage house stands was named for him.

Union general James H. Wilson moved into Overlook when his troops occupied Macon in 1865. From the veranda the Yankees could clearly watch the progress of Reconstruction. In 1887, the former Confederate president Jefferson Davis and his family were entertained here.

When George Woodruff and his family's foundations donated one million dollars to Mercer University to renovate the mansion in 1993, its name was changed in his honor.

Those renovations were in progress when Sgt. Wood arrived.

She closed and secured the huge front door, then walked through the first floor of the mansion, her footsteps echoing in the emptiness. She felt

WOODRUFF HOUSE TODAY

goose bumps rise on her arms, but she wasn't cold. When she tiptoed up the grand stairs to the bedrooms for her tour and inspection of the house, the feeling grew more intense. She had never felt this way before in all her years of duty, and she didn't know what to make of it. Her intuition told her to run out the front door and never come back, but she knew she couldn't abandon her post.

Her recollection of Col. Bond's tragic death didn't quiet her fears—he had been murdered by his plantation overseer.

A March 15, 1859, account in the *Macon Telegraph* recorded Col. Bond's death:

> A misunderstanding had subsisted for some time between Col. Bond and Lucius Brown, formerly his overseer, but now employed on a neighboring plantation, owned by Col. Beall. Brown had a short time before, unjustifiably assailed and severely whipped an old and faithful servant of Bond's; and on Saturday morning, Col. Bond examined the injuries sustained by the servant, and finding them to be very severe, became excited to a frenzy.

Bond mounted his horse and starting after Brown found him on horseback on Beall's premises, assailed him with a stick and knocked him off his horse. Brown, recovering his feet, shot Bond through the body, whereupon Bond dismounted and fired at Brown as he ran from him, wounding him in the thigh. Bond lived but thirty minutes after the rencontre. Another statement of the facts attending the rencontre is that after unhorsing Brown, Bond dismounted and was in the act of pummeling Brown with his stick when the latter discharged his pistol.

The remains of Mr. Bond were brought to this city on Sabbath last, and on Monday, interred in Rose Hill Cemetery, escorted by the Bibb Cavalry, (of which Company he was a member) and followed by a large concourse of citizens.

Col. Bond was much esteemed in this community. He was an influential and enterprising citizen and urbane gentleman. He leaves behind him a large circle of attached kindred and friends to mourn his tragic fate. His immediate family have the sympathies of our entire community under this crushing and irreparable bereavement.

Mrs. Bond lived alone in the mansion for twenty years until her death in 1879.

Sgt. Wood suspected that the unsettled spirit haunting the house might well be Col. Bond, so she decided to confront him head on. She stood directly in the center of the front hall, amid all the plaster dust and discarded wood mouldings, and called out to him: "All right, Col. Bond. I'm here whether you like it or not. I'm here to protect your house from thieves and vandals. I will not harm your house. Mercer University is restoring your house to its original beauty. We are doing nothing to destroy the house in any way. I am not leaving."

At first she felt uncomfortable calling out into the empty darkness, but after a few minutes she felt certain this is what she had to do. She explained to Col. Bond the plans for the house and how it would be used. There was only silence in return, and she continued to sense an atmosphere of hostility, so she called again. "Col. Bond, I'm here to protect your house. I'm here to protect you. If I don't stay, vandals will break in like they did last week."

For a second she thought she heard him say, "I didn't like all those kids in here," and the response startled her. She wondered if he meant a time in the 1960s, when the mansion housed the Stratford Academy, the first private school in Macon for grades one through twelve, founded when integration began.

After that brief exchange there seemed to be some relief in the level of anger. She experienced the strong hostility only in some of the rooms.

On subsequent nights, as soon as she entered the house, she immediately said, "Good evening, Col. Bond. I'll be here until eight a.m." After the second night she didn't feel quite so foolish doing this; by the third night the greeting seemed very appropriate. The tactic seemed to work, because after the third night the hostility disappeared, and warmth greeted her for the next three months.

Upon completion of Sgt. Wood's stay at the Woodruff House, an alarm system was installed with outside amplifiers on the roof. The alarm began activating three to four times a night, greatly disturbing the neighborhood and law students. Finding no real explanation for the malfunction, the alarm company removed the outside amplifiers in hopes of putting a stop to the problem, but to no avail—the alarm continued to sound.

After several nights of this, Sgt. Wood began to think that since nothing mechanical seemed to be wrong with the alarm, the perpetrator might be Col. Bond. That night she went to the house to confront the ghost. Telling him that she knew he was setting off the alarm, she added, "Mr. Bond, this has to stop! I will not be back. You must not set the alarm off anymore."

Except in times of power failure and severe weather, the alarm has worked perfectly since then. Says Sgt. Wood, "I can only assume Mr. Bond became used to my being in the building every night and when I stopped being there that upset him."

Col. Bond apparently remained quiet until one night when a psychic attended a meeting at the house. She was about to descend the stairs when she fell, bruising her knees and tearing her stockings. She swore she was pushed by a strong hand, yet no one was near her.

On another occasion, after a meeting in the southeast parlor, one lady stayed behind to check some of the details in her accounts. She was sitting on the sofa and looked up to see a tall, dark-haired man in a tall, gray felt hat looking at her from the other side of the coffee table. Curiously, he was dressed in a waistcoat and trousers, garb of the 1860s. She couldn't imagine who it could be, as she had locked the door after all the other people left. When she asked, "May I help you?" he vanished.

One of the security guards who worked in that area for about twenty years admitted that he'd seen Col. Bond several times and on two occasions had spoken to him. He confirmed that he was dressed in clothing of the 1860s, but he described him as an old man.

The same security guard saw another puzzling phenomenon in the house: he watched a lady in a long black dress float up and down the grand stairs. He says that he's seen the same woman in Willingham Chapel, another Mercer University building.

The home is open to the public on the Christmas tour. For information contact University Relation and Development, 1400 Coleman Ave., Macon, GA 31201, or Macon-Bibb Co. Convention & Visitors' Bureau, Terminal Station, 200 Cherry St., Macon. Call the Visitors' Bureau at 912-743-3401.

WILLINGHAM CHAPEL

Ofc. John Morgan, a policeman working the midnight-to-eight shift at Mercer University, was in Willingham Chapel at about two o'clock one morning when he heard the sound of footsteps that seemed to be coming from the balcony echoing throughout the chapel. They sounded as if they were treading on wood, but the floors in the balcony are made of concrete. After searching the area, he found no one. He knew that he had locked the chapel doors behind him when he arrived, and he knew that he possessed the only key. He wondered how the mysterious person could have entered or left without being detected. There were panic bars on the doors that might have facilitated an escape, but he hadn't heard them open.

That same night as he walked through the auditorium in the basement of the chapel, Morgan ran into a column of freezing air. Startled, he walked all around the area and noted that the air surrounding the pillar was quite warm by comparison. He stepped into the frigid column, but the cold air became intolerable, and he had to back away.

These unusual occurrences brought to mind old rumors of a Confederate soldier or officer who may have been killed there in the 1860s. Stories of an apparition seen by some students in the early 1900s still circulated.

Or could this be the ghost that Mercer's drama students call Oscar? Mercer University's tiny Back Door Theater inhabits the chapel basement and, according to an article in the *Macon Telegraph*, October 28, 1994, one night in the mid-1970s a student who was rehearsing for a play was nearly clobbered by a large wooden plank that apparently fell from nowhere. All of the doors in the theater were locked, and the student was quite sure he was alone in the building. When he investigated, he discovered that the

THE ENTRANCE TO WILLINGHAM CHAPEL AT MERCER UNIVERSITY

timber matched similar pieces found in the *attic* of the old building.

How could this particular piece have mysteriously fallen onto the stage? After much discussion and conjecture, the most popular explanation was that the near-tragic accident had been the prank of a ghost. From then on, the drama students attributed all mysterious occurrences in the building to the ghost they dubbed Oscar.

Paul Oppy, Mercer's theater director since the fall of 1974, denies the existence of the ghost. He says that the incidents happened to the students, not to him, and while he enjoys hearing their stories, he remains a skeptic.

According to Oppy, the students believe that Oscar's pranks have been numerous. During the first dress rehearsal of each new play, Oscar seems always to play with the lighting. Sometimes props disappear when they are needed most. Some students admit that they feel a "presence" from time to time in the chapel and the theater.

According to the newspaper article, one student, Shelly Johnson, recalled a time when she and another student were alone, rehearsing their lines in the chapel. They heard a seat in the chapel creak, followed by the sound of a door closing, but they never saw anyone leave. Johnson said that she felt the "presence" in the theater dressing room and refused to be there alone. "This place is like a labyrinth," the article quoted her as saying. "It's dark and moldy, and there's lots of little passageways and cubbyholes. It gets scary."

Paul Oppy doesn't think there's anything to worry about. "From all of the students' reports, Oscar is not a malevolent ghost," Oppy says. "Oscar appears to be more of a trickster."

For information about performance schedules, write the Back Door Theater, Mercer University Office of Speech and Drama, 1400 Coleman Avenue, Macon, GA 31207, or call 912-752-2974.

THE VICTORIAN HOUSE

The owner of a lovely 1890 Victorian home on Peachtree Street in Macon was born in the house and has shared it with a spirit as long as she can remember. When she was a little girl, she'd wake up and feel as if someone were standing in her bedroom, yet no one was ever there. Her grandmother said it was just her imagination.

When I went to interview her for this book, I had no idea that I would become a part of the story and actually provide her an opportunity to "see" the spirit that she has known for so long.

In any event, as she grew older in the house, other unusual things began to happen, usually in the early spring. She might sense a presence in the room and then smell the scent of a fresh rose. Or she might encounter a cold spot in the living room. Or she might be reading in bed and glimpse a figure passing quickly by the door.

"I know when she's about by the action of my dogs," the woman says. "They refuse to go into the hall, and their fur stands straight up across their backbone. Sometimes they'll hover at the door and bark at the empty hallway. I tell them to be quiet, because it's only the 'lady.'"

About fourteen years ago the spirit apparently became rather playful. The bathroom light began to switch on, apparently by itself, in the middle of the night. When the lady of the house went to bed the light would be off, yet when she awoke in the morning the light would be shining brightly. She consulted an electrician and replaced the light switch, but the strange phenomenon continued—the light persisted in turning itself on.

One night she couldn't sleep and was sitting in bed reading when the bathroom light came on by itself about three o'clock. By that time she'd

THIS UNRETOUCHED PHOTOGRAPH BY THE AUTHOR CAPTURED AN IMAGE OF SOMETHING ON THE PORCH. IS IT THE SPIRIT OF THE YOUNG WOMAN WHOM THE OWNER SENSES LIVES HERE?

decided that the "lady" was behind the prank, so she yelled, "Damn it! Cut that out!" The light winked out immediately and has never caused any trouble since.

For years the lady has been notorious for moving small objects from one place to another. Keys left on the dining room table may be found the next morning on the buffet.

The owner tells us that her mother has seen the lady up close. One time when her mother was visiting she was having a problem with her back and decided that she would be most comfortable sleeping on the sofa in the living room. During the night she awakened and saw a figure standing in an open doorway. She later described the figure as a female, about five-foot-five, thirty years old, with long, dark hair and wearing a white robe or gown.

THESE BLURRED PHOTOS ARE FROM THE NEGATIVES THAT
IMMEDIATELY FOLLOW THE PHOTO ON THE PREVIOUS PAGE. DO
THEY "PROVE" THAT THE IMAGE IN THE FIRST PHOTO IS A GHOST?

She was puzzled, and reported that she observed her a good long time. Finally deciding that it had to be her daughter, she called out, "Dear, is something wrong?" The moment she spoke, the figure disappeared. The door, which had been open when she first saw the figure, was tightly closed and chained shut from the other side.

The owner's mother, who now lives in the house with her daughter, is from time to time awakened in the middle of the night by the dogs barking at something in the hallway. Yet each time, no one or nothing is there.

The owner has never seen the lady, but there are times when she senses the presence of someone standing behind or beside her, which raises the hair on the back of her neck. Once she picked up a message from her that said, "In an old piece of furniture, there's a large amount of money." The words entered her mind seemingly from out of the blue when she felt the presence near. She did search the house, but she never found the money.

She isn't afraid of the lady and thinks of her as part of the family.

ABOUT THE PHOTOGRAPHS

When I took the photographs that illustrate this chapter, I had no idea the lady was on the porch. The owner of the house and I were both amazed at the resulting image, and the owner, once she regained her speech, says that she now feels that she knows for sure who caused all the odd little incidents in the past. We tried to take another picture but the spirit didn't cooperate.

The owner of the photo shop in Milledgeville that developed the film was fascinated when he saw the picture of the ghost, and he brought another phenomenon to our attention. It has been noted, he says, that when supernatural energy is photographed, the pictures in the next two frames on the roll don't turn out well. In this case the next two pictures are, indeed, spoiled.

When the negatives were returned to the dark room for duplicates, the technician had great difficulty getting a clear image. She had to repeat the process three times before she was able to reproduce the ghost print, yet she had no problem with any of the other prints in that batch.

The Victorian house is a private residence and not open to the public.

PIEDMONT
&
TIDEWATER

GHOSTS AT TIFT COLLEGE

Ghosts seem to haunt and linger around locations where death occurs during some great adversity. Perhaps they are attached to the site, to the land, and when a new structure is built, they move in. Apparently they roam about, rattling doors and creating other disturbances, even in buildings that didn't exist at the time of the tragedy. So it is in Forsyth, Georgia, near Atlanta, where the Forsyth Collegiate Institute served as a Civil War field hospital in 1864 and 1865.

Wounded soldiers were transported to Forsyth by train, and many of the college students nursed them during this time of great stress. For two years the campus was a place of tragedy and death, spawning numerous ghosts who still reside on the campus even though it has undergone numerous physical changes over the years.

THE CIVIL WAR FIELD HOSPITAL

Ella Palmer was a nurse who followed her husband, Confederate general Joseph Benjamin Palmer of Tennessee, from battle to battle during the Civil War. Ella and her staff came to Forsyth to set up a field hospital to care for the wounded in anticipation of the battle of Atlanta which occurred in late June 1864. She left the following account in her journal:

> Finding no suitable houses in Forsyth, the hospital tents
> were pitched in a beautiful grove just back of the town [now
> the campus]. The work that was involved can be imagined
> as all the tents were floored and trenches were dug around
> each one. A scientific man belonging to the corps found a

bed of pottery clay and as all kinds of vessels, dishes, etc., were becoming very scarce this proved a great boon to the hospital. [There is a kaolin deposit on modern Highway 83 nearby.] A potter was speedily found and a large furnace built which was run night and day until the need was more than supplied.

The Hospital had hardly become settled and in good running order when the battle of Stone Mountain occurred. The next morning the trains came in bearing the wounded. Most of the injured men of this battle were sent to the Ford [hospital in Atlanta].

It was well that the hospital was in a grove for it had tents for only 1200 men and they already had 800 on hand. Over 1000 men were brought off these trains. These were hauled out to the hospital in ambulances and wagons and laid under the trees. The need was so great that the people of Forsyth went to work and helped to bring them out to the hospital in their carriages and wagons. These good people tore up their sheets and tablecloths to make bandages and brought bedding and other necessary things to the hospital. The physicians of the town came and offered their services, which were gratefully accepted. The surgeons had their operating tables placed out under the trees.

Many soldiers died in the hospital, marking the spot for all eternity as one where extreme suffering was experienced by many.

THE LEGEND OF HONORA SWENEY

Near the campus lie the graves of 299 Confederate heroes and one brave young woman, Honora Sweney. According to legend she was one of the

Forsyth Collegiate Institute students who stayed on to nurse the soldiers. She contracted typhoid fever, and when she recognized that she would not survive, she asked to be buried anonymously, with the soldiers who fought so valiantly and died so painfully. She was buried according to her wishes, in a grave marked simply "Confederate."

A SINGLE MARKER

The grave of James A. Darter, a member of Camp 24, Texas Regiment, is the only one of the 300 graves identified with a name. A comrade in battle, Bob Neal, wrote to Darter's family of his injuries and his subsequent death. After the war, Darter's brother sent a marble monument to be placed over James's grave. The monument stands in the center of the plot and towers over the others.

AFTER THE WAR

The Forsyth Collegiate Institute reopened after the war, becoming the Monroe Female College in 1871. In 1879 a fire completely destroyed all of the buildings. Some buildings were restored in 1883 after funds were accumulated for that major task, and the name was changed to Tift College to honor Bessie Willingham Tift, whose husband was an outstanding benefactor of the institution. Tift Hall, a dormitory built in 1903, became the major source of ghostly sightings on campus over the years.

THE GHOST OF BESSIE TIFT

In its span of nearly seventy years, Tift Hall was home to thousands of women students and a ghost named Bessie after the school's benefactress. Many a night the spiritual Bessie could be heard walking up and down the long, dark corridors, her heels tapping as she moved from door to door,

TIFT HALL WAS TORN DOWN IN 1971.

stopping briefly to rattle the knobs.

If a student dared to open the door, all she found was emptiness and silence. But when the door closed, the tap, tap, tapping could again be heard echoing down the hall as the ghost moved on.

Besides her nocturnal prowling, there were many other stories of ghostly activity, reports that Bessie was heard walking up the stairs, stories of doors that opened mysteriously, water faucets that turned off and on by themselves, and the sounds of footsteps and breathing outside the students' doors.

Legends abounded. Some of the students suspected that the ghost might have been a nurse at the Confederate Hospital—perhaps Honora Sweney—who found a lover among the wounded, a lover who didn't survive and is buried in the graveyard on campus. Might the young girl have died grieving for her lover? Perhaps each night her sad spirit returned hoping to find her lover.

FACES IN A WINDOW

In 1971-1972, Tift Hall was razed and replaced with a modern building. Someone from the history department supposedly snapped a photo before the antiquated building was torn down, just minutes before the bulldozers arrived. Although the building was locked and completely vacant at the time, the faces of two young men looking out of two different windows appeared in the photo. In a college newspaper, the photographer asked, "Could they be ghosts from the Civil War?"

The picture was so impressive that it was enlarged to mural size and was dislayed in the lobby of Lies Hall until the college closed in 1987. Neither the mural nor the photo can be located today, but reports exist, and two former students of Tift College swear to have seen the photo.

An account in the October 1973 issue of the *Campus Quill,* the student newspaper, mentioned the mural:

> Have you ever studied the picture of the old Tift
> Dormitory in Lies Dorm? If you look closely at the windows
> you can see two faces peering out. That picture wasn't
> taken until after Tift Hall was vacated.

"The faces appeared to be of two young men aproximately 16 or 17," claimed a former student who was familiar with the mural. "Their faces weren't clear like photos, but filmy and slightly transparent. It sent chills up my spine to think their spirits were still here."

RESILIENT SPIRITS

When Tift Hall came down, the students wondered what would happen to Bessie and the other ghosts. Would they disappear with all the mortar, trusses and white columned porches? Much to their great relief, Bessie apparently survived. The *Campus Quill,* in the December 1971 issue, reported:

> There was a ghost who kept opening the suite door in
> room 59 in Tift. In West Dorm now, every night Mary Nell
> Harris's door opens by itself. Or does an unseen hand open
> it?
>
> At 7:15 a.m. every morning while they were living in
> Tift Hall, Sandra Burnette and Gail Davidson heard a noise

that sounded like a man walking down the halls—step, drag, step, drag, step, drag. When they went to investigate, there was nothing there. They tried several times to see who made the noise, but they were never successful.

In West Dorm, a few weeks ago after Gail and Sandra had retired for the night, Sandra felt something push her bed. When she asked Gail if she was in bed yet, Gail looked toward Sandra's bed and something black was standing over Sandra. Was it their visitor from Tift?

Several other reports of ghosts surfaced and were reported in the *Campus Quill* on October 29, 1973. In Lies Hall, a relatively new building, another ghost was discovered. He was called Jefferson, the soldier boy of Lies dorm. Some people suspect he died in the field hospital and his spirit now searches for peace.

Whatever the story, one thing is clear—the spirits of the soldiers who died there still abound, as they probably have for more than 130 years. Tearing down the buildings hasn't changed their habits at all, and their presence seems to prove once again that a building doesn't need to be old to be haunted. The spirits seem to linger on or near the location of their death no matter how the area changes, stuck somewhere in the astral plain between heaven and earth, maybe for all eternity.

Ebon Academy now uses the old Tift College campus as a private boarding school for exceptional children. It is not open to the public.

PANOLA HALL

In Eatonton, Georgia, the name Panola Hall, which means cotton in the Choctaw language, conjures up visions of white columns and southern antebellum opulence. Even a mere glimpse of the mansion proves it is so—but what can't readily be seen is the ghost of a young woman who has lived there for the past 130 years. The beautiful girl has stirred the hearts of many who have seen her. Louise Hunt, who lived here in the late 1800s, named her Sylvia after a popular song of the day, and was moved to write a poem about her. She tried—unsuccessfully—to prevent a northern millionaire, a frequent guest of the Hunts, from falling in love with her. But Sylvia's story starts even earlier.

THE TRIPPE FAMILY

An enterprising young man from North Carolina, Henry Trippe, married Elizabeth S. Perry on May 9, 1836. They prospered as planters in Putnam County, Georgia, where Trippe was a highly respected and responsible citizen. In 1854 he contracted James M. Broadfield and Tunis Tunison to build a mansion for his lovely wife and two growing daughters, Mary, then fourteen years old, and Louisa, age nine.

The 1860 census for the county, the only record available after the war, lists only Henry Trippe, 55; Elizabeth, 56; an unnamed son, 14; John Trippe, 85, identified as a farmer in North Carolina; and Henry Trippe, Sr., 74, also from North Carolina. The two daughters, who would have been ages 20 and 15 are not listed. Had they passed away in an epidemic of some kind? Or had they died in an accident? The elder may have married and moved away,

PANOLA HALL AS IT LOOKS TODAY

but there are no records to prove this. Their absence from the census roster remains a mystery that may never be solved. Some think the lovely spirit of Sylvia may be one of the Trippe daughters.

A CONFEDERATE BELLE

Rumors of another beautiful southern belle have fostered other speculations about Sylvia's identity. Some think she was a friend of the Trippe family who was visiting during Sherman's brutal march to the sea and fell in love with one of the Confederate soldiers who escaped capture by hiding at the plantation. Legend has it that ten or twelve of them stowed away in two tunnels that lie beneath the house—one that led to a well in the front yard and another that ran under downtown Eatonton all the way to the courthouse. Later, as the story goes, when the young woman heard that her lover had been killed, she was devastated. Inconsolable in her grief, she threw herself over the second floor balcony and died in the front hall. Perhaps this unfortunate young woman is the elusive Sylvia.

RECENT CONFIRMATION

In 1979 a resident found three mid-19th century weapons—a musket, a shotgun and a sword—jammed down between the outside wall and inside plaster lath in a remote location in the attic. The current owner uncovered several loose musket balls in the same area. This discovery has reinforced the long-held suspicion that Confederate soldiers actually hid in the house. The discovery of a concrete chamber with a vaulted ceiling beneath the house also reinforces this theory. With its obscured entrance, it is unlikely that a search party would find the 7' x 14' vault unless they knew exactly where to look.

THE HUNT FAMILY

When Henry and Elizabeth Trippe died, their descendants rented the mansion to the family of Dr. Benjamin Weeks Hunt of New York, a scientist, horticulturist and banker who fell in love with a girl from Eatonton, Louise Reid Purdon, and married her in New York. Because his wife longed for the South, in 1867 they settled in Putnam County with the fifty registered Jersey cows that he brought with him. The Hunts bought the mansion in 1891 and named it Panola Hall.

Georgia was still under Union occupation, but Hunt was able to use his expertise to help other farmers, together developing Putnam County into the dairy capital of Georgia. He introduced Bermuda grass as a successful forage crop and was responsible for establishing the first rabies treatment facility in Georgia, following his own near-fatal bout with what he thought was the disease. With no local help available at the time, he had to travel all the way to Paris for treatment. In 1922 the University of Georgia awarded Hunt an honorary degree of Doctor of Science.

Apparently the Hunts saw Sylvia often but rarely spoke of her. Mrs. Hunt wrote a poem about the girl, and after his wife died, Dr. Hunt read it to visitors. It can be found in *Brown's Guide to Georgia*, December 1979.

An Ode to Sylvia

Sylvia's coming down the stair—
Pretty Sylvia, young and fair
Oft and oft, I meet her there,
Smile on lip and rose in hair.

From her dim and dusty room
Flits she in the twilight gloom,
And I breathe a faint perfume
Of a damask rose in bloom.

Musky perfume floating where
Winds and twists the quaint old stair
Well I know the look of her,—
Hand light laid on bannister.

Garments of the days that were
But her garments make no stir
As she glides by. Light as air
Fall her footsteps on the stair.

Stand aside, and let her pass—
Little room she takes, alas.
Sylvia died, they tell me so
Died a hundred years ago;

Yet, she meets me, I declare.
Oft upon the winding stair.
Pretty Sylvia, young and fair—
Though I'm old, I'm debonair.

When I feel her presence nigh,
And she smiles as she glides by,
Then I lift to her my hat,
Could a man do less than that?

In the *Eatonton Messenger* in 1960, Mrs. Hunt is quoted as telling the postmistress,

> I first saw Sylvia when I was sitting here in the library. I looked up and saw this beautiful girl leaning over the bannister of the stairs and laughing at me. I jumped up and said, "Who are you and how dare you laugh at me in my own house?" She laughed at me again and then came gliding through the room, still laughing, and disappeared into thin air.

Mrs. Hunt didn't tell her husband about the ghost until someone else saw it, a friend who was visiting from Ohio, thought to have been a millionaire named Nelson. He met Sylvia as he was on his way upstairs one afternoon and later described her as a beautiful young woman dressed in a white hoopskirt and wearing a damask rose in her long, dark hair. Nelson stood close to the wall to let her pass by. She smiled at him and bashfully inclined her lovely head to one side as she floated down the steps with her hand barely touching the banister. The scent of roses lingered in the hall after she'd vanished—to another room, he thought.

Nelson was surprised when the young woman didn't appear for dinner. When he saw that the table was set for only three, he asked the Hunts about the charming lady he'd met on the stairs. His hosts told him that he'd just met Sylvia, their resident ghost. So struck was he with her beauty and poise that he didn't believe them. He thought they were playing a trick on him. As time passed he reluctantly accepted their explanation, but to him Sylvia remained quite real. So real, in fact, that he wrote many love letters to the ghostly sweetheart. He suggested that Mrs. Hunt open the letters and leave them on the dresser in the room where Sylvia had disappeared from view. He hoped that Sylvia would read the letters and know of his love for her.

The newspaper account of the incident concludes, "There is no record of what happened to those epistles of ghostly love, although the story is authentic." A subsequent owner reported that he understood that the mysterious Nelson had eventually died in a coldwater flat in New York, disowned from his family for unknown reasons and penniless. But his last wish was to be buried with a copy of Sylvia's poem in his hand and placed just above his heart. He was still in love with her.

Alice Wardwell, the Eatonton librarian for many years, once spotted Sylvia from afar without knowing it. One quiet summer evening Mrs. Wardwell went outside to sit on the front step and enjoy the sunset. The library, built in 1913 and endowed by the Hunts, was directly across the street from Panola Hall. An article in the Eatonton *Messenger* on July 20, 1989, gives Mrs. Wardell's recollection of an incident that probably occurred in the 1920s:

> Through the open windows of their living room I could see Dr. and Mrs. Hunt as clearly as though they were on a lighted stage. Mrs. Hunt was busy with some sewing or some fancy work and Dr. Hunt was reading.
>
> At once I was struck by a strangeness about the scene. Dr. and Mrs. Hunt had a visitor to whom they were paying absolutely no attention. The visitor was a beautiful, dark-haired young woman wearing a long white dress, and she stood directly behind Dr. Hunt's chair, as though reading over his shoulder.
>
> Why, I wondered, were Dr. and Mrs. Hunt ignoring her so completely? They were the most gracious, the most hospitable people in the world. Yet, not once did Dr. Hunt raise his eyes from his book, nor Mrs. Hunt look up from her sewing.
>
> About that time children came up the walk with books to return. "Children," I said casually, "look across the road and tell me what you see." One of the young girls said, "They've got company. Look at the young lady standing behind Dr. Hunt."

Alice Wardwell asked each of the children in turn, and each of them saw Sylvia. The next day she asked Dr. Hunt who his visitor had been. He was surprised at the question, and when the librarian described the young girl she had seen, he admitted that it must have been their ghost. It seems as if he hadn't seen her that time.

A long-time friend of Mrs. Hunt's, a Miss Butler, was interviewed by the *Atlanta Journal* magazine in the December 14, 1941, issue:

"I had heard about Sylvia for many years," said Miss Butler, "but never expected to see her, as I am a practical sort of person and ghosts just don't register with me. It was the afternoon of Mrs. Hunt's last illness (1929). I went across the hall from my room into a guest room to see if it was in readiness for relatives we expected on the next train.

"The only people in the house at the time were Dr. Hunt and the nurse at Mrs. Hunt's bedside downstairs, and the cook in the kitchen. I was the only person upstairs.

"I had walked into the center of the guest room and was taking a swift glance about when, from the corner of the room behind me, came the sound of someone tiptoeing.

"Then a sweet beautiful voice called sadly, 'Miss Bessie. Oh, Miss Bessie.' Just that and no more, but it was enough . . . I ran past the white blur in the corner that I knew to be Sylvia, but I didn't want to see her."

According to another report in the *Brown's Guide to Georgia*, December 1979, Wink Walker, a young man who was riding his bicycle past Panola Hall one day in the 1950s, saw a wispy, tall something cross the outside steps, go diagonally into the house and through the closed door. "I went running home and told my two older brothers," he said. On another occasion many years later, he entered the attic from the upstairs bedroom to read the electric meter. When he came back down he spotted a pair of shoes behind the door, and when he closed it, he was surprised to see the filmy form of

IN THIS UNRETOUCHED PHOTO TAKEN BY THE AUTHOR, A WISP OF
WHITE MIST CAN BE SEEN AGAINST THE SHUTTER, A SPOT WHERE
SYLVIA HAS REPORTEDLY BEEN SEEN MANY TIMES.

Sylvia in the corner.

Mr. and Mrs. M. L. Liles operated a boardinghouse at Panola Hall in the 1960s. In 1969 Mrs. Liles reported infrequent ghostly activity, but they had trouble with the lights going on and off at the most inconvenient times. An even more annoying problem was a constant drip, drip, dripping noise upstairs. It drove them crazy—so much so that Mrs. Liles insisted that her husband tear up the floor and fix the leak. He did as she asked but found absolutely nothing wrong with the plumbing.

One of the boarders who lived in the right front bedroom upstairs claimed that someone pulled the blankets off him at night. This prank happened so often that he finally jumped up one night and said, "Sylvia, stop it this instant!" From that moment on he never had any more trouble with his blankets.

Elaine Hodges, now an emergency room physician, was only ten when she persuaded her friends to join her in going "trick or treat" at Panola Hall. They had all grown up with the stories of Sylvia and weren't afraid of her they said, but that made the expedition all the more adventuresome.

The others hung back on the front steps as Elaine knocked on the heavy front door, calling "trick or treat!" in a trembly voice. The children all watched spellbound as a hand passed between the curtains and the glass at the window next to the door. Immediately, they all screamed and ran, until halfway down the walk Elaine recovered, convincing herself that it was only Mr. Liles trying to trick them. Turning, she walked back to the door and defiantly knocked while the others waited on the walk.

After a few seconds, Mr. Liles opened the door. "Mr. Liles, we saw a hand pass by the glass there in front of the lace curtain just a minute ago. That was you just fooling us, wasn't it?" Elaine asked.

Mr. Liles looked puzzled. "I don't know what you're talking about. I've been sitting there in the library watching the news. What did it look like?"

When Elaine described it as a "lovely young girl's hand, soft, smooth and pink," she and Mr. Liles stared at each other in surprise. "It must have been Sylvia," he said.

When Mr. Liles was very ill and near the end of his life, Sylvia appeared to several people. A neighbor even admitted seeing Sylvia cross her lawn and enter her house. The people of the neighborhood wondered if she was upset by the renovations which were also occurring at the same time as Mr. Liles's illness.

The present owner, Dr. Robert Lott, felt drawn to Panola Hall the first time he saw the mansion while passing through Eatonton. In 1980, almost ten years later, he stopped when he saw Mr. Liles sitting on the front steps and asked if he wanted to sell Panola Hall. Dr. Lott didn't know it, but the mansion had been on the market for more than a year.

Dr. Lott, who is renovating the mansion, has become infatuated with Panola Hall and Sylvia. Although he claims never to have seen her, he feels her presence as a warmth and hospitality that permeates the old mansion, the feeling that first drew him to the spot. "It has a certain chemistry," he says, "like meeting an old friend for the first time."

Several years ago, when his mother was visiting, she thought she heard footsteps in the hall. Their Doberman barked frantically at the closed bedroom door, but when his mother opened it no one was there. On another visit his mother was entering her bedroom when she saw a figure standing behind the chair in the corner. At first she thought it was her son and called to him, but the figure stooped down behind the chair and hid. When she walked over to investigate, the figure had vanished. His mother was sure it was Sylvia, Dr. Lott says.

A VERY RECENT SIGHTING

The mansion was empty when I arrived to take some pictures in April 1995. A caretaker was kind enough to let me in. I couldn't help wondering what had become of Sylvia. Was she still there as Dr. Lott said? Was she gazing quietly out the window on cold mornings and floating up and down the stairs? Did she wander in the empty library and yearn for the more exciting years?

After I had taken all of my pictures, I lingered on the stairs calling, "Sylvia, Sylvia, Sylvia." To my great surprise, I heard an answering whistle—a small whistle, a child's feeble attempts at practicing his first sounds through pursed lips. I heard it four times. When I questioned the caretaker, he replied that he'd never uttered a peep.

I wanted to believe that the whistler was Sylvia. I returned to the landing and again listened carefully. That time I heard the faint cries that sounded like small kittens in the parlor below. I wondered if she was trying to tell me about the little babies. I didn't understand the message, but I felt sure I knew who the messenger was.

And when my pictures were developed, thin swirls of gossamer appeared near the shutter in the guest bedroom—Sylvia's room. I felt sad knowing that she hadn't passed on. Dr. Lott admits that he loves Sylvia, too. "How could you not love her?"

Panola Hall is not open to the public, but can be seen on Madison Avenue in Eatonton.

EBENEZER SWAMP

The story of the ghosts of Ebenezer Swamp in southeast Georgia dates from the Civil War, but even today folks will admit that on dark, dreary nights, when the stream is swollen from the winter rains, moans and cries for help from the hysterical victims—more than a thousand men, women and children—can still be heard echoing in the swamp's mists. Who are they? Victims of a ruthless Northern army that let them drown.

Part of General William T. Sherman's Union army marched for several weeks to reach Camp Lawton, the Confederate prisoner of war camp just outside of Millen, Georgia. Reports had filtered northward that the conditions there were as bad those reported at the infamous Andersonville Prison or even worse. Witnesses had allegedly seen a ten-acre yard containing ten thousand men with no facilities for shelter or comfort inside a stockade fence of stout tree trunks. Sherman, believing this inaccurate report, vowed to free his men from this prison.

In truth the camp covered forty-two acres, and the ten thousand men brought there from prisons in Savannah when the camp was finished early in November of 1864 were only there for several weeks. The Yankee prisoners were treated well by their Confederate captors; there was good, pure water available and a daily ration of cornmeal, cooked beef, salt and rice. When word reached the camp that Sherman was marching toward town, all of the prisoners were moved farther south for safekeeping.

In December, when the Union army finally arrived, they were furious to find the camp deserted. So incensed was Sherman that he ordered his soldiers to burn the entire town of Millen to the ground, including the prison camp stockade. The local folk fled for their lives to neighboring towns.

As Sherman again headed southward, his army attracted two thousand black refugees seeking their freedom. Men, women, and children followed in wagons, on horseback and on foot, carrying bundles on their heads and babies in their arms. To them this was the beginning of the glory road to freedom, and they didn't want to miss it.

Beyond Guyton, they marched through three miles of "the most fearful swamps." One division was forced to halt entirely. Heavy winter rains had turned the roads to mud, and twenty-four wagons sank to their beds. They also lost several mules, who simply sank out of sight. Much to their dismay, they found that the Confederates had destroyed the bridge over Ebenezer Creek, a larger-than-normal stream that was swollen to overflowing. It was a hundred feet wide where the army decided to cross and ran very deep, so the commander ordered the soldiers to construct a pontoon bridge.

Despite the added confusion of Confederate cannon that sporadically shelled the Union troops, and Confederate gunboats that fired onto the road from their positions on the Savannah River, Ebenezer Creek had to be crossed. Jim Miles, in his recent book entitled *To The Sea,* described the crossing: "At midnight word was passed down the line to advance in absolute silence. The fourteen thousand Yankees filed across Ebenezer Creek through a dark, dismal rain."

Union general Jefferson C. Davis was concerned that the black contrabands would hinder the corps' ability to deploy and fight, and he had tried to turn them back earlier. Now they were forced to stand off the road, in the swamp, awaiting their turn to cross. A division commander later reported that the crossing "had been a delicate undertaking for the route traversed a mile of the most gloomy, dismal cypress swamp I ever saw, on a narrow causeway, just wide enough for a wagon to drive along."

When the last Yankee touched down on the eastern bank of Ebenezer Creek, General Davis, warned that a Confederate regiment had been spotted in the area and was about to attack and unmindful of the waiting blacks, gave orders to disengage the bridge immediately. Having done so, the Yankees prepared to depart the area to make ready for combat.

Two thousand black refugees were left stranded on the west bank. Believing that the Confederates would certainly shoot them all for running away should they be caught, fear and panic filled the slaves, and without a moment's hesitation desperate men, women with babes in their arms and helpless children plunged into the swift, angry current. Hundreds of them drowned.

Many of the Yankees continued to move out of the area, ignoring the screams for help from the drowning victims, but some took pity on the dying and threw pieces of wood for them to grab. Several soldiers felled trees in an effort to provide a rough crossing. One soldier later recalled seeing a giant black man pull a log raft back and forth across the river, carrying pitifully few refugees to safety.

Long into the afternoon the cries of the victims sounded in the swamp. Drowned bodies filled the stream to the banks like logs in a jam, until one by one the current pried them loose and carried them away downstream.

Tragically, most of the refugees perished unnecessarily. The recaptured slaves weren't shot, but simply returned to their owners.

Ebenezer Swamp is on Route 17, about six miles from Rancon, Georgia, just north of Savannah.

COL. GEORGE W. FISH

Although the house he built in 1852 was moved from Oglethorpe to Americus in 1969, the ghost of Col. George W. Fish, who died a violent death in 1871, still lingers within its walls.

The colonel was a judge of the district court and one of Macon County's distinguished citizens. Before his death at age 51, he was very interested in literature and the arts, the cultivation of fruits and flowers for the decoration of his home and the town. Many of the exotic trees and shrubs in Oglethorpe today were planted by him.

The following is excerpted from an account in the *History of Macon County* published in 1933:

> John Holsenback felt that Col. Fish had wronged him and was determined to get revenge. Jim Loyd, the man Holsenback lived with, advised him to kill the colonel at once. Holsenback saw Col. Fish board a train for Macon and knew Fish would return on the evening commuter.
>
> Holsenback was waiting behind the stairs in the courthouse when Col. Fish approached. Fish was fired upon and died almost instantly. Holsenback fled to his friend's house. Loyd was waiting for him and asked, "Did you get the wolf?" John calmly replied, "Yes."
>
> After the coroner's verdict of murder, John Holsenback followed the body to Col. Fish's house on the lovely spring morning in 1871. Holsenback even helped place the corpse of his victim in the casket. Mrs. Fish knelt in front of the casket and prayed that the assassin would come forward

COL. FISH'S HOUSE, BUILT IN OGLETHORPE IN 1852, WAS
MOVED IN 1969 AND NOW STANDS IN AMERICUS.

and touch Col. Fish. When Holsenback overheard the prayer, he quietly disappeared.

The town was in an uproar for days as they tried to find the murderer. Finally, Rufus B. Bullock, the governor of Georgia at the time and a friend of Col. Fish's, sent two detectives by the name of Rasberry and Murphy to investigate the case.

Murphy thought to test Holsenback by staring at the man and stating, "John Holsenback, you committed that murder," but Holsenback was so frightened by the direct statement that he confessed immediately. Loyd was arrested at three o'clock the next morning after they had compared the gun wadding from his own supply with that in Col. Fish's gun.

The detectives converted a goods box into a washstand and put it in one of the jail cells with the open side next to the wall and hid inside it beforethe prisoners were brought in.

The next morning Rasberry and Murphy jumped out from behind the washstand and confronted the two murderers with all the facts that they had divulged during the night. On June 28th they were convicted of murder, and although they appealed three times to the governor for leniency, they were refused each time. They were both hanged eventually, and people came from miles around to witness the event.

Even though there was justice in the end, Col. Fish's spirit walks in his house to this day. Mr. and Mrs. Donald Nelson had the house moved to Americus in 1969. Apparently Col. Fish's spirit became angry and restive during the move, causing some delays in the project. The builders originally intended to complete the work at night, but so many mysterious things happened that they resorted to working only during the day. Sand and mortar boxes were upset, windows were broken, ladders tipped over, tools mysteriously fell, and other odd occurrences delayed their progress. When the house was situated in Americus, other little accidents that hampered progress assured them that the colonel's presence was still there.

After a time the house was restored to its original beauty, and the Nelsons moved in and set up housekeeping. A story in the *Macon Telegraph and News,* August 5, 1973, reported the following incident:

> Mr. Nelson was dozing by the fire when he was aroused by a lean, dark-haired man dressed in period clothing. "I was not really asleep," said Nelson. "He told me he had been very upset about the house being moved. However, since we were restoring it to his liking, he was happy and peaceful."

Dr. Gatewood Dudley, who bought the house from the Nelsons, said that

THE REMAINS OF COL. GEORGE W. FISH AND HIS WIFE LIE
BENEATH THESE ELABORATE TOMBSTONES IN OGLETHORPE.

Col. Fish's presence was strongest in the book-lined front parlor and that
one received a definite sensation upon sitting in a red velvet eighteenth-
century English tub chair that Mr. Dudley referred to as Fish's chair, even
though it was never owned by the colonel. "Col. Fish was a scholarly
gentleman," Dudley observed. "He should be happy with all these books.
Shakespeare's his favorite, I think, and oh, of course—his red velvet
chair."

*A private residence currently owned by Mr. & Mrs. Randolph Jones, the
Fish House is not open to the public.*

THE OLD FARM

One night in the 1980s some teenage boys with time on their hands and no definite plans went for a drive in the country. As they drove they entertained themselves with ghost stories. This wasn't unusual; they often told each other stories, each one scarier than the next.

One boy related a supposedly true, tragic story of an old farmer in Baxley who was riding his tractor in the field one clear September day, plowing up the earth for the fall seeding of rye grass and holding his precious granddaughter on his lap. She was his pride and joy and he took her along every chance he could, just to be with her. The farmer and the child laughed together as they bumped up and down over the large clods of earth, but the vibrations and noise from the motor were such that they could barely hear themselves speak.

Suddenly and unexpectedly the tractor lurched into a gully, and the child slipped from the old man's arms. He grabbed for her and tried to stop the engine at the same time, but his efforts were to no avail. The tractor lurched forward, and the child was dragged beneath the machinery. The old man heard her screams above the engine noise and struggled frantically to reach her, but it was too late—the child was dead.

The old farmer was so distraught that he left his farm and never returned. Some said that before he died, he went crazy from his grief.

The boys had heard that his ghost haunted the old farm and since they were in the area, they decided to find it. They searched several deserted country roads and finally arrived at a farm they thought was the one in the story. They laughed and joked nervously, reassuring one another that it was just a story, but all four were still a little nervous as they got out of the car and walked cautiously and silently up the lane.

The moon had risen slightly behind the abandoned clapboard house, and in the steely moonlight they spotted an old, rusted tractor in the middle of an overgrown field. A chill shot up each spine. Could this actually be the place?

One boy broke the silence. "This isn't the place," he whispered. "It must be farther down the road." Relieved that the tension had been broken, they turned to go back to the car but were suddenly brought up short when they heard the sound of a door closing and a screen door slamming shut. They whirled about, but the boarded-up house had no screen door, and no one was in sight. They heard the sound of footsteps crossing the planks of the sagging front porch, but still they saw no one.

As they stood transfixed in the lane, the weeds in front of the tractor rustled and waved in the still air, as if something—or someone—were walking toward the machine. Suddenly the night was filled with the sound of a tractor engine trying to turn over, groaning and grinding until finally it caught and roared to life, as if an unseen operator were ready to go to work.

The boys were petrified. They stared at the derelict tractor frozen in the field, and although it never moved, they clearly heard the sound of it moving around and around the field, straining at times, as if it were plowing up the thick sod.

Then suddenly the tractor's motor revved, and they heard the sounds of a child screaming, yet still nothing moved. The tractor sat frozen in its track. The baby continued to scream as they turned and fled to their car. The screams stopped just as they jumped into it.

The boys raced toward home as fast as they could, and they never returned to the spot of the terrible tragedy. To this day each one swears that this story is true.

Baxley, Georgia, is 31 miles south of Vidalia on Route 1.

FORT MCALLISTER

The garrison at Fort McAllister, located just below Savannah on the Ogeechee River, relied for its main defense on massive walls covered with huge mounds of river mud, sand, and sod that concealed large bomb shelters, called "bombproofs" underneath. The enemy cannonballs were swallowed up by the sod-covered embankments, defying destruction of the fort.

During the War Between the States, Ft. McAllister withstood seven attacks by the Union forces from both the rice fields in the rear and the river in front. Between attacks, garrison life could be fairly quiet, giving the men time to think about their situation.

TOM CAT

The garrison at Ft. McAllister, like many Confederate camps, adopted a mascot to help relieve their loneliness. Their mascot was Tom Cat, a coal black cat who was fed and cherished by everyone. The men denied the usual association of black cats with bad luck and fiercely protected the animal.

According to reports from Confederate diaries, during the assaults Tom Cat ran back and forth along the grassy wall, dodging the cannon and musket balls that flew overhead until he was finally killed by a stray shot on March 3, 1863.

The day Tom Cat was killed the fort survived seven hours of intensive bombardment by the Union gunboats *Passaic, Nahant* and *Patapsco.* These gunboats were supported by the assaults of cannon blasts from nine more

A RECENT PHOTOGRAPH TAKEN AT FT. MCALLISTER SHOWS THE
ENTRANCE TO A BOMB SHELTER. TOM CAT RAN ALONG THE
GRASSY TOP OF THE BERM DURING ATTACKS ON THE FORT.

Union ships located one to two miles offshore. Despite the ferocity of the attack, the only Confederate casualty reported that day was Tom Cat. The death was deeply regretted by all the men and a full report of the fatality was communicated to General Beauregard in the official report of the action.

Now the fort is open to the public, and a plaque has been erected to Tom Cat's memory. Visitors and reenactors in the garrison have spotted a swift black cat running through the rooms. At times they've seen him racing across the high turf mounds, stopping for several seconds to get a glimpse of the river, then racing on over the walls, as if late for an appointment.

Sometimes just the edge of his tail is seen turning a corner, or the high arch of his back appears in the shadow of a cannon. The reenactors have felt his presence at certain tense moments; many have seen his black face, intently scouting out the enemy, while others have sworn they felt his warm back rub against their bare leg.

The managers of the fort deny that there is a cat on the premises, but many others feel certain that the spirit of Tom Cat is still on duty, patrolling the mounds after all these years.

MAJOR JOHN B. GALLIE

Major John B. Gallie was mortally wounded while commanding the eight-inch artillery at Fort McAllister during a seven-day siege in February 1863.

According to the records, a Union ironclad had approached and taken a position within eight hundred or a thousand yards of the battery to the north. The Union wooden ships lay about two miles away to the east. The enemy fired steadily and with remarkable precision, aiming at the eight-inch Columbiad, an immense cannon located atop of the huge earthen mounds of the fort.

The Columbiad could reach a target of from one to three miles away, so the enemy was anxious to render it inactive. Within a half hour the parapet in front of the gun was so badly damaged that the entire gun was exposed. Major Gallie had been wounded in the face by a fragment of shell, but refused to be relieved. He continued his duties in spite of his suffering, inspiring his men with his own gallant and unconquerable spirit.

Then Major Gallie was mortally wounded by an enemy shell that hit him directly in the head. The official report says it caused a wound that exposed his brains. Some say that he was scalped by the blast, others say that he was beheaded. In any event he died that day from his massive wound and was mourned by all for his unwavering gallantry.

Sometime in the 1960s some of the groundskeepers from the fort reported a very strange incident. One February morning, about the time of day that Major Gallie died, the men were trimming the grass around the Columbiad when an icy chill surrounded them and an eerie quiet descended over the fort. They looked to the river to see if a storm was brewing, but the sky was sunny and cloudless. They then saw the form of a headless body hovering for several minutes over the spot where Major Gallie had been mortally wounded. The ghost faced out to sea, as if scanning the river for gunboats. The crew claimed that the ghost was dressed in a dark blue militia uniform with an officer's braid on the sleeves. Many Confederate soldiers wore dark blue militia uniforms early in the war before gray became available.

Some claim that the headless ghost resembled the long dead Major Gallie. Others insist that no ghost ever existed and the stories are the confabulation of wild imaginations. But in the early morning hours, when the full moon hangs on the horizon, as it did the day Major Gallie was killed, no one wants to venture onto the point of Fort McAllister to see for himself.

The Ft. McAllister Historic Park in Richmond Hill is open Tuesday through Saturday, 9:00 to 5:00, and Sunday 2:30 to 5:30. Camping facilities are also available. For more information call 912-727-2339.

FORT PULASKI

The garrison at Fort Pulaski on Cockspur Island in the Savannah River was taken over by the Yankee general Quincy Gillmore on April 11, 1862. From October of 1864 until March of 1865, the Union used the garrison as a prisoner-of-war camp.

The Yankees used every measure to win the war, even if it meant violating the military code of ethics. They put six hundred prisoners from Fort Delaware into a one and a half acre stockade on the beach during the prolonged battle of Morris Island in 1864, hoping that the Confederates, who were trying to regain control of the island, would hesitate to fire on their own men.

Miraculously, not one prisoner was killed during the six weeks of battle, thus earning the prisoners their famous sobriquet—the Immortal Six Hundred. When the prisoners were moved back to Ft. Pulaski, they suffered all manner of abuse. By the end of the war, thirteen of them had died and been buried in unmarked graves outside the fort.

During a memorial ceremony on March 18, 1994, a group wanting to remember these heroes placed a simple laurel wreath over their graves in a gesture of homage. Later that evening, when all of the participants of the ceremony were supposedly inside the fort for the night, Nicholas, a twelve-year-old boy wandering the grounds, observed a solitary Confederate soldier in a gray uniform with gold scroll braiding on his sleeves, kneeling in prayer in front of that wreath, his hat in his hand. The boy approached the soldier, but when he didn't recognize him as one of the reenactors, he stopped dead in his tracks. The soldier turned and walked away, his image fading in the twilight gloom. The boy couldn't believe his eyes and ran back

THE ENTRANCE TO FORT PULASKI, WHERE THE MYSTERIOUS
CONFEDERATE SOLDIER STOOD GUARD

into the fort to tell his story.

When the boy reported his experience, the men in Confederate uniforms were queried as to their activities. It was determined that no one other than the boy had been outside the fort for at least an hour. The stunned reenactors decided that the man must have been one of the Immortal Six Hundred, praying for his friends. The experience reaffirmed for them the importance of their mission to commemorate these valiant souls.

THE SENTRY AT FORT PULASKI

On a recent visit to Fort Pulaski a mother and her son spoke to a sentry dressed in a Confederate uniform who stood guard beside the massive front gate. After some conversation about how old his sword looked and how unique his musket was, they asked him where the restrooms were. He said that he'd be happy to show them but regretfully he couldn't leave his post.

A little while later they stopped a ranger on the other side of the fort and asked him for directions. He pointed back toward the front gate and said the restrooms were near the entrance. With some irritation she informed the man that the sentry over there had refused to tell them the location of the restroom. "He claimed that he couldn't leave his post," she said.

The staff member was puzzled. "There's no one on duty over there," he told her. "We don't have soldiers dressed in Confederate uniforms at the fort."

Both mother and child assured the ranger that they had, indeed, spoken to a Confederate sentry beside the front gate, but when they all returned to the spot, the sentry had disappeared.

For further information about the fort, write Fort Pulaski National Monument, P.O. Box 30757, Savannah, GA 31410, or phone 912-786-5787. The park is open seven days a week from 8:30 to 5:15.

BIBLIOGRAPHY

MILLEDGEVILLE

The Governor's Mansion
Beeson, Leola S. *The One Hundred Years of the Old Governor's Mansion, Milledgeville Georgia, 1838-1938.* Macon, GA: The J.W. Burke Co., 1938.

Hines, Nellie Womack. *A Treasure Album of Milledgeville and Baldwin County, Georgia.* 1949. Reprint. GA: McGaw Laboratories, 1974. (Hereafter *Treasure Album.*)

Perkerson, Medora F. *White Columns in Georgia.* New York: Bonanza Books, 1927. (Hereafter *White Columns.*)

The Homestead
Henson, Calvert. "Middle Georgia Ghostly Sampler." *Macon Magazine,* Vol. IV, No. 1. November-December 1989: 60-64.

Strickland, Binky. "Terrorizing Tales." *Union Recorder* 26 October 1990: 6, 8. (Hereafter "Terrorizing Tales.")

White Columns.

The Tate House
Schemmel, Bill. "The Ghost and Miss Katherine." *Georgia* October 1973: 46-47, 75-76.

"Terrorizing Tales."

White Columns.

Major Edward White House
Cook, Anna Maria Green. *History of Baldwin County.* Spartinbury, SC: The Reprint Co., Publishers, 1992. (Hereafter *Baldwin County.*)

The Old State Capitol
Baldwin County.

Treasure Album.

The Spirit of the Burial Mounds
Baldwin County.

Memory Hill Cemetery
Archer. "Ghost Stories." *Macon Telegraph* 31 October 1991: 1A-8A.

_____. "Ghosts Stay Busy in Milledgeville Cemetery." *Macon Telegraph*
31 October 1991; 1A-8A.

Leach, Lauren. "Strange Powers That Be." *Union Recorder* Vol. 176, No.
216. 29-31 October 1994: 1A, 12A.

Michaelsen, Johanna. *The Beautiful Side of Evil*. Eugene, OR: Harvest
House, 1982.

"Terrorizing Tales."

Georgia College

Hair, William I., James C. Bonner, and Edward B. Dawson. *A Centennial
History of Georgia College*. Milledgeville, GA: Georgia College, 1979.

_____. *A History of Georgia College*. Milledgeville, GA: Georgia College,
1979.

The Old State Prison

Duffey, Barbara D. "Milledgeville's Old State Prison." *Middle Georgia
Magazine* Vol. 3, No. 4, 1993: 19-23.

The Ghost of Marion Stembridge

Dobson, Wanda. "The Stembridge Murders." *Middle Georgia Magazine*
Vol. 4, No. 1, Spring 1994: 66-68.

Sears, Steven M. "Murder-Suicide Shocked Milledgeville." *Union
Recorder* Vol. 175, No. 87. 1-3 May 1993: 1A-12A.

MACON

The Hay House

Beasly, David. "Hay House Alive." *Atlanta Journal Constitution* 2 March
1986: 2H, 4H.

Jones, Tommy H. *The Johnstons, Feltons, & Hays*. Macon, GA: The
Georgia Trust for Historic Preservation, 1993.

Knifflin, Joy. "Hay House 'Ghost' Sends Out Messages." *Saturday
Telegraph and News* 2 May 1981: 1B, 4B.

McInvale, Morton Ray. "Macon, Georgia: The War Years, 1861-1865."
Thesis, Florida State University College of Arts and Sciences, June
1973.

Smith, Terri K. "Are There Ghosts at the Hay House?" *Macon Telegraph
and News* 31 October 1984: 1D, 3D.

White Columns.

The Beall House

Census Reports: 1860, 1870, 1880 Georgia and 1870 Macon

"Downtown Macon Fired." *Macon Daily Telegraph* 2 February 1865: 2.

Macon Directories: 1865, 1866, 1868, 1870, 1875, 1899.

Martin, John H. *Columbus, Georgia, from Its Selection as a "Trading Town" in 1827 to Its Partial Destruction by Wilson's Raid in 1865.* Columbus, GA: Thomas Gilbert, 1874.

Wright, Buster W. *Columbus (Georgia) Enquirer* 1832-1872, c. March 1984: index to *Columbus, Ga.*, 12.

The Woodruff House

"Death of Col. Joseph Bond." *Macon Daily Telegraph* 15 March 1859: 1.

McKay, John J., and Nellie Edwards Smith. *A Guide to Macon's Architectural and Historical Heritage.* Macon, GA: Macon Historical Society, 1972.

Payne, Calder W. *Rose Hill Rambles.* Macon, GA: Penfield-Rowland Printing Co., for Middle Georgia Historical Society, 1985.

Willingham Chapel

Smith, Sharon. "Spooky Tales to Help You Have a Happy Halloween." *Macon Telegraph* 28 October 1994: 1A, 8A.

PIEDMONT & TIDEWATER

Ghosts at Tift College (Forsyth)

Adams, Myrna. "Bessie Now Hauntless." *Tift Cornerstone*, Alumni Bulletin, Vol. 1, No. 2. Spring 1972: 44.

Garrison, Sherry. "Ghosts Walk Campus." *Campus Quill* Vol. 40, No. 3. December 1971.

"Ghosts Haunt Hallowed Halls." *Campus Quill* Vol. 42, No. 2. 29 October 1973: 5.

"Historical Sketch of Bessie Tift College." *Chiaroscuro*, Tift College yearbook. 1926: 17.

Patton, Jessie Williams. "Unknown Grave Marks a Tift Legend." *Tift Cornerstone*, Alumni Bulletin, Vol. 2, No. 1. Summer-Fall 1972: 6.

Stone, Eugenia Wootton. *Yesterday at Tift.* Doraville, GA: Foote & Davies, 1969.

Panola Hall (Eatonton)

Georgia Census 1850, 1860 Henry Trippe Family

Joslyn, Mauriel. "Bizarre But True: Sylvia, the Socially Discerning Ghost." *Middle Georgia Magazine* Vol. 4, No. 1. Spring 1994: 20-21.

"Librarian Alice Wardwell Recalls Summer Appearance by Sylvia the Ghost." *Eatonton Messenger* 20 July 1989, 7.

Putnam County Historical Society. *Marriages and Wills in Putnam County,*

1830-1860.

"Sylvia Lived Here: Some Folks Say She Still Does." *Brown's Guide to Georgia Magazine* December 1979: 68-70.

"Terrorizing Tales."

"Today Panola Hall's Sylvia Hasn't a Ghost of a Chance." *Atlanta Journal Constitution* 19 February 1969.

White Columns.

Ebenezer Swamp (Effingham County)

Joslyn, Mauriel Phillips. *For Retaliation: The Story of Six Hundred Confederate Officers and the United States Prisoner of War Policy.* Shippensburg, PA: White Mane Publishing, 1995. (Hereafter *For Retaliation.*)

Miles, Jim. *To the Sea: A History and Tour Guide of Sherman's March.* Nashville, TN: Rutledge Hill Press, 1989. (Hereafter *To the Sea.*)

Miller, Frances Trevelyan. *Prisons and Hospitals: A Photographic History of the Civil War.* 1911. Reprint. New York: Thomas Yoseloff, Inc., 1957.

Page, James Madison. *The True Story of Andersonville Prison: A Defense of Major Wing.* New York: Neal Co., 1908.

Col. George W. Fish (Oglethorpe & Americus)

Cook, Jacquelyn. "Ghost Sits in Red Velvet Chair." *Macon Telegraph and News* 5 August 1973: 2C.

Hays, Louis Frederick. *History of Macon County, Georgia.* Atlanta, GA: Stein Printing Co., 1933.

Fort McAllister (Tidewater)

Official Records—War of the Rebellion of the Union and Confederate Army. Vol. XIV Series I, Chap. XXVI: 212-217.

To the Sea.

Fort Pulaski (Tidewater)

Coulter, Merton E. *Georgia: A Short History.* Chapel Hill, NC: University of North Carolina Press, 1947.

For Retaliation.

To the Sea.

Roberts, Robert B. *Encyclopedia of Historic Forts: Military Pioneer and Trading Posts of the United States.* New York: MacMillan, 1988.

INTERVIEWS

Andrews, Louis H., Milledgeville.
Campbell, Paul, Milledgeville.
Cannon, Randy, Milledgeville.
Cheek, Kevin, Macon.
Edmonds, Charles, Milledgeville.
Flanders, Lorene, Milledgeville.
Fowler, Katherine, Milledgeville.
Gibson, Fr. & Mrs. Robert, Macon.
Hodges, Becky, Atlanta.
Hodges, Elaine, Eatonton.
Jarvie, Greg, Ph.D., Milledgeville.
Jennings, Sibley, Macon.
Jones, A. Alling, Milledgeville.
Jones, Mr. & Mrs. Randolph, Americus.
Joslyn, Mauriel, Sparta.
Joslyn, Nicholas, Sparta.
Joyce, Marvin, Milledgeville.
Kidd, Culver, MIlledgeville.
Kitchen, Renee Padgett, Milledgeville.
Kugaraj, Krista, Norcross.
Lott, Robert, Eatonton.
May, Paul & Mary Ann, Milledgeville.
Mead, Greg, Macon.
Morgan, John B., Juliette.
Olivier, Ray, Milledgeville.
Simpson, Ken & Tine, Milledgeville.
Smith, Alma, Milledgeville.
Spear, Edward, Milledgeville.
Stoneking, Darin, Milledgeville.
Tate, Mary Barbara, Milledgeville.
Webb, Reba, Milledgeville.
Weber, James A., Macon.
Wilson, Robert, Milledgeville.
Wood, Pat, Macon.

INDEX

B

Back Door Theater 77, 79
Baldwin Hotel 42
banshee 6-7, 10
Beall House, The 61-67
Beall, George 61-62
Beall, Martha 61
Beall, Nathan 61-62, 73-74
Bivins, Stephen T. "Pete" 46-48
Bond, Col. Joseph 72-76
Boykin Plantation 14
Brown, Lucius 73-74
bugler 22
Bullock, Rufus B. 105
burial mounds 23
Burnette, Sandra 89

C

Campus Theater 47
Central State Hospital 23, 26, 39, 42
chieftain 23
Civil War 1, 4, 6-7, 17, 20, 21-22,
54-55, 61-63, 65-66, 72, 77, 85-87, 89,
90, 92, 93, 102-104, 111-114, 115-117
Colquitt, Julia Hurt 63
Cooper, Johnny 43-44
Cowles, Jerry 72
Crucifixion (mural) 37
Culver Kidd Drugstore 39-41

D

D'Assaro, Danielle 58
Darter, James A. 87
Davidson, Gail 89
Davis, Chester 57-58
Davis, Jefferson 54, 72
Davis, Jefferson C. 103
Dillard, Alice 12, 14
Dudley, Dr. Gatewood 107-108

Dunlap, Ilah (see also Jordan,
Leonidas) 63-64

E

Ebenezer Swamp 102-104
Ebon Academy 90
Ennis, Marion 44, 47-48
Evans, Frank 45

F

Felton, Ellen Tracy 55
Ferguson, Fanny Way 6
Ferguson, Frances 6, 8
Fish, Col. George W. 105-108
Fish, William 24
Forstmann & Co. 36
Forsyth Collegiate Institute 85, 87
Fort McAllister 111-114
Fort Pulaski 115-117
Frank, Leo M. 36

G

Gallie, John B. 113-114
Gardner, Martha 63
Georgia College 1, 29-31, 32-33, 34,
42, 48
Georgia Military College 21-22
Gillmore, Quincy 115
Governor's Mansion 1-5, 21
Griffin, Dr. George G. 61
Griffin, Juliet Beall 61-62

H

Harris, Mary Nell 89
Hay House, The 51-60
Haygood, Dixie 25-27
Holsenback, John 105-106
Homestead, The 6-11
Hunt, Dr. Benjamin Weeks 93, 96
Hunt, Louise Purdon 91, 93, 95, 97

I

Indian burial mounds 23

J

Johnekin, Emma 44-45
Johnson, Shelly 79
Johnston, Ann Tracy 53-54, 56
Johnston, Caroline 54
Johnston, Edward Tracy 53
Johnston, Francis Campbell 53
Johnston, Mary Ellen 54
Johnston, Susan Mary 53
Johnston, William B., Jr. 53
Johnston, William Butler 53-54
Jones, John "Honest Jack" 7
Jordan, Leonidas A. (also see Dunlap,
Ilah) 61-64

L

La Farge, Fran 55, 57-60
Lies Hall 89-90
Liles, M. L. 98-99
Loyd, Jim 105-106

M

Maj. Edward White House 17-19
Memory Hill Cemetery 7, 24-28, 36
Mercer Law School 14
Mercer University 72, 74, 76-79
Milledgeville Penitentiary 29
Milledgeville State Prison 36-38
Miner, Bill 36
Monroe Female College 87
Muskhogean Confederacy 23

N

National Historic Trust 55
Native American chieftain 23
Neal, Bob 86
Nelson, Donald 107

O

Oconee Town 23
Old Farm 109-110

Old State Capitol 20-22
Old State Prison 36-38
Oppy, Paul 78-79

P

Palmer, Ella 85
Palmer, Joseph Benjamin 85
Panola Hall 91-101
Parke, Lucinda 6
Phagan, Mary 36
Pons, Dr. Leon 37

R

Random House 12
Richard Binion Clinic 44
Rose Hill Cemetery 63, 74
Russell Auditorium 29-31

S

St. James Church 68-71
Sanford building 47, 49
Sanford Hall dormitory 29
Scott, Katherine 12, 14-15
Sherman, William T. 1, 20, 30, 55, 62,
92, 102-103
Smith House, Ann Simpson 32-33
Smith, J. R. 40
Smith, Molly 2
Spirit of the Burial Mounds 23
Stembridge boardinghouse 42, 48-49
Stembridge, Marion 42-49
Stratford Academy 75
Sweney, Honora 86-88

T

Tate House, The 12-16
Terry, Sam 43-45
Tift College 85-90
Tift Hall 87-89
Tift, Bessie Willingham 87-89
Tom Cat 111-113
Trippe, Elizabeth Perry 91, 93
Trippe, Henry 91, 93
Trippe, John 91

Trippe, Louisa 91
Trippe, Mary 91
Trolley Tour (Milledgeville) 16, 19, 22
Turner, Ike 4

V

Victorian House, The 80-83
Vinson Hall 22

W

Walker, Joe 12, 14
Walker, Molly 12, 14
Walker, Sam 12-14
Walker, Wink 97
Wardwell, Alice 96-97
Watts, Jimmy 45
Webb, Reba 41
White House, Maj. Edward 17-18
White, Catherine 17
White, Dr. Benjamin Aspinwall 17-18
White, Edward II 17
White, Maj. Edward 17
White, Samuel Gore 17-18
Wilkinson Street House 34-35
Williams, Lucinda 7
Williams, Peter J. 6
Williams, Sue 7-9
Willingham Chapel 76, 77-79
Wilson, James H. 55, 72
Woodruff House, The 72-76
Woodruff, George 72

DO YOU HAVE A GHOST STORY TO TELL?

If you have a true ghost story you'd like to share with author Barbara Duffey, you can contact her at the address below:

Barbara Duffey
c/o Rockbridge Publishing Company
P.O. Box 351
Berryville, VA 22611

Outstanding stories will be considered for inclusion in Ms. Duffey's next book, but no story will be published without the express permission of the storyteller.